2—

ROB FEENIE

photography by **JOHN SHERLOCK**
food styling by **NATHAN FONG**

FEENIE'S

BRUNCH · LUNCH · DINNER

DOUGLAS & McINTYRE
Vancouver/Toronto/Berkeley

To the "Feenie Family": my incredible parents,
Margaret and Laurie; my dear wife, Michelle;
our beautiful son, Devon, and our newest member,
"Feenie-to-be." Here's to a lifetime of stories!

Douglas & McIntyre Ltd.
2323 Quebec Street, Suite 201
Vancouver, British Columbia
Canada V5T 4S7
www.douglas-mcintyre.com

Library and Archives Canada Cataloguing in Publication
Feenie, Rob, 1965–
Feenie's : lunch, brunch, dinner / Rob Feenie.

Includes index.
ISBN-13: 978-1-55365-135-2   ISBN-10: 1-55365-135-9

1. Cookery. 2. Feenie's (Restaurant) I. Title.
TX945.5.F42 F42 2005   641.5'09711'33   C2005-903522-6

Library of Congress information is available upon request.

Editing by Saeko Usukawa and Lucy Kenward
Cover and interior design by Peter Cocking
Photography by John Sherlock
Food styling by Nathan Fong
Printed and bound in Canada by Friesens
Printed on acid-free paper
Distributed in the U.S. by Publishers Group West

We gratefully acknowledge the financial support
of the Canada Council for the Arts, the British Columbia Arts
Council, and the Government of Canada through
the Book Publishing Industry Development
Program (BPIDP) for our publishing activities.

CONTENTS

ABOUT FEENIE'S

FOR ME, opening Feenie's was a dream come true. At my first restaurant, Lumière, I wanted to make a statement. That's the arena where I try to push the limits of my capabilities and test the rules of dining. At Feenie's, my intention is to introduce guests to some of my favourite places around the world and to translate the dishes into a language that speaks of Canada. If Lumière is one bold statement about who I am as a chef, then Feenie's is the story of my life.

During my time as a young chef at Le Crocodile here in Vancouver, my dear friend Michel Jacob took me to Alsace and fed me buttery tartes flambées, briny choucroute and smoky sausages. I found that I loved these simple, beautiful dishes prepared by a master chef. This was comfort food that told me stories about where my friend had come from. I wanted to know more.

In my travels, I have been lucky enough to visit some of the most well-respected chefs around the world. Each has their own unique style, but with every dish I've tasted, I've learned another story. The flavours that stayed with me are the ones that speak of the surrounding regions and local products.

Now, with *Feenie's* cookbook, I offer you my own collection of stories. Here are my memories of rich onion soups at Au Pied de Cochon in Paris, heavily laden charcuterie boards in Roman cafés, and hot dogs from street vendors in Sweden, all brought back home to Canada and re-created with our finest local products.

In August 2004 I got the call to be the first Canadian chef to do battle on *Iron Chef America*. It was such an honour to go head to head against Masaharu Morimoto, who in my opinion is the true Iron Chef. That competition was the most difficult test of my abilities I have ever had to endure—and to win was definitely the highlight of my twenty-one-year career. It was not only a triumph for me personally, but a testament to the talent of all Canadian chefs.

I am really pleased to be able to share my travels and experiences with you. Perhaps these dishes will bring back memories of stories for you, too.

ROB FEENIE

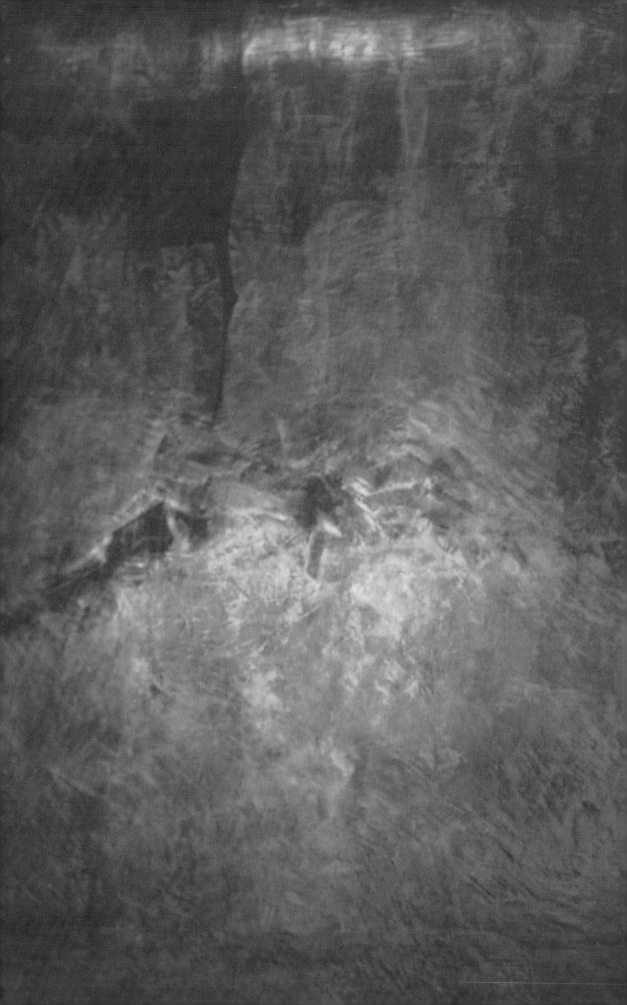

FEENIE'S BRUNCH

STEAK AND EGG

JUS

¾ cup dry red wine, such
as a Shiraz-Cabernet blend

⅓ cup port
(your favourite kind)

½ cup finely sliced shallots

¼ head garlic, halved

2 sprigs fresh thyme

5 cups veal stock (page 134)

STEAK, EGG AND
ASPARAGUS

4 rib-eye steaks (each 8 oz)

¼ cup extra-virgin olive oil

24 stalks asparagus

1 tsp unsalted butter

1½ cups red wine jus

4 large eggs

Chopped chervil, for garnish

THIS IS a brunch dish, but it also has become one of the most popular dinner items at Feenie's. When I was growing up as a kid, I had the good luck to have this dish regularly. When you buy the steak, look for some fat marbling in the meat, as that's what gives it both flavour and tenderness. And you can freeze the leftover red wine jus; it is a tasty all-purpose sauce for beef or veal. *Serves 4*

JUS: Combine wine, port, shallots, garlic and thyme in a large saucepan on medium heat. Cook for 15 to 20 minutes, or until reduced to a syrup. Add stock and cook for about 45 minutes, or until reduced by one-third. Strain. Makes about 3 cups. Will keep in the freezer for 2 months.

STEAK, EGG AND ASPARAGUS: Preheat the oven to 375°F. Season meat with salt and freshly ground white pepper. Place a large ovenproof frying pan, or possibly two (you don't want to crowd the meat, so make sure there is lots of room) on high heat. Add 1 Tbsp of the oil to each pan. When oil is lightly smoking, sear steaks for 1 to 1½ minutes on each side, or until browned. (If you like your steak "blue," meaning really rare, remove from the pan now and serve.) For medium-rare steaks, place the frying pans in the oven and cook for 10 minutes. Remove from the oven and transfer steaks to four warmed plates. Allow meat to rest while you prepare jus, asparagus and eggs.

Fill a bowl with ice water. Bring a saucepan of salted water to a boil. Cut off and discard woody bottoms of asparagus. Blanch asparagus by cooking in the boiling water for 2 minutes, then take out asparagus and plunge it immediately into the ice water to stop the cooking (this preserves the colour and flavour).

Heat butter and ½ Tbsp of the oil in a large frying pan on medium to medium-high heat. Add asparagus and sauté for 2 to 3 minutes. Remove from the stove, then season with salt and freshly ground white pepper.

Bring jus to a boil in a small saucepan on high heat, then remove from the stove.

Heat 1 Tbsp of the oil in a nonstick frying pan on low to medium heat. Add eggs and cook for about 3 minutes, or until the whites are no longer transparent.

TO SERVE: Place 6 asparagus stalks on top of each steak. Drizzle the warm red wine jus over steaks. Top each serving with an egg and drizzle with the remaining olive oil. Garnish with chervil.

SOUFFLÉD APPLE PANCAKES

WITH CINNAMON MAPLE SYRUP

BRUNCH IS ONE of the most exciting sections on the Feenie's menu. We are free to play with food that reflects the more relaxed atmosphere of a lazy weekend afternoon, and it is the one meal when we can offer dessert as a main course. This recipe achieves that level of sinfulness. Indulge in this fabulous dish, then go for a long afternoon stroll. *Serves 4 to 6*

MAPLE SYRUP: Place all the ingredients in a saucepan on high heat and bring just to a boil. Remove from the stove and allow to cool. Store syrup, with the spices in it, in a jar in the refrigerator. Will keep for 4 months.

APPLES: Melt butter in a large frying pan on medium heat. Add brown sugar and stir until dissolved. Cook for 3 minutes until bubbly. Add apples and cook for about 8 minutes, or until softened. Remove from the heat.

PANCAKES: Mix together eggs and sugar in a large bowl. Add flour, milk, vanilla, salt and cinnamon, then whisk well. In small batches, process in a blender until frothy. Strain through a fine-mesh sieve.

TO ASSEMBLE: Preheat the oven to 425°F. Divide apples into four 8-inch (or six 6-inch) ungreased casserole dishes. Ladle the pancake batter into the casseroles (1½ cups for each 8-inch dish or 1 cup for each 6-inch dish). Bake in the oven for 7 minutes. Rotate the dishes 180°, then bake for another 7 minutes, until golden brown and puffed.

TO SERVE: Place each casserole on a plate. Garnish each serving with a dusting of icing sugar. Serve with a jug of cinnamon maple syrup on the side.

MAPLE SYRUP

1 quart maple syrup

3 sticks cinnamon

6 whole star anise

APPLES

⅓ cup butter

⅔ cup brown sugar

7 Granny Smith apples, peeled, cored, ¼-inch dice

PANCAKES

10 large eggs

5 Tbsp sugar

1¾ cups all-purpose flour

2½ cups milk

1½ tsp vanilla extract

¾ tsp salt

½ tsp ground cinnamon

Icing sugar, for garnish

LOBSTER EGGS BENEDICT

LOBSTER HOLLANDAISE

1½ lb whole live lobster

2 egg yolks

½ cup water

1 cup clarified butter (page 136)

1 Tbsp fresh lemon juice

4 Tbsp chopped fresh chervil

EGGS BENEDICT

¼ tsp white vinegar

8 eggs

4 English muffins

1 cup mixed-herb salad (equal amounts of chervil, chives and parsley)

ONCE, ON A TRIP to Fiji several years ago, I had lobster with poached eggs and hollandaise sauce for breakfast. If you've never had this before for breakfast or brunch, you will just be crazy about it as I am. *Serves 4*

LOBSTER HOLLANDAISE: Bring a stockpot of water to a boil on high heat. Add lobster, cover the pot with a lid and boil for 2 to 3 minutes. Transfer lobster to a platter and allow to cool. Remove meat from tails and claws. Cut meat into ¼-inch dice.

In the top of a double boiler on medium heat (or in a bain marie, which is a bowl set in a pan of very hot water), whisk together egg yolks and water until light in colour, fluffy and slightly thickened.

Place clarified butter in a saucepan on medium-low heat and warm it up. Slowly add clarified butter to the egg mixture, whisking all the while. Fold in lobster meat. Stir in lemon juice, then season to taste with salt and freshly ground white pepper. Keep warm in the double boiler (or bain marie) while you poach eggs.

EGGS BENEDICT: Fill a deep frying pan with an inch or two of water and bring to a rapid simmer on medium heat. Add vinegar. Break each egg into a cup. Gently slip one egg into the simmering water, stirring the water gently to form a whirlpool to help shape egg into a neat oval (the vinegar will also help the egg whites to set). Cook the egg for about 3 minutes, until the white is no longer transparent. Use a slotted spoon to transfer the egg to paper towels to drain. Repeat the process for each egg.

TO SERVE: Slice English muffins in half, then toast lightly. Arrange two halves on each of four warmed plates. Place a poached egg on top of each muffin half. Stir chervil into the lobster hollandaise and spoon over each egg. Garnish with herb salad on the side.

MUSHROOM AND
GOAT CHEDDAR OMELETTE

ERE ARE A FEW TIPS on how to make a good omelette. First, buy a good nonstick frying pan and use it *only* to cook omelettes. Never cook anything else in it, ever. And do not wash it, just wipe it with paper towels after each use and give it a quick rinse. Second, cook omelettes on medium heat and do not overcook them—there should be little or no browning.

Chèvre noir is a mature Cheddar type of goat cheese from Quebec. You can use any sharp old Cheddar instead. *Serves 4*

MUSHROOMS: Melt butter in a large frying pan on low heat, being careful not to let it brown. When butter is foaming, add mushrooms, season with salt and sauté for about 5 minutes, or until cooked. Stir in shallot and cook for 3 to 4 minutes. Season with freshly ground black pepper, parsley and chives. Keep warm.

OMELETTE: Whisk together eggs and cream in a bowl. Season with salt and freshly ground white pepper.

Melt butter in a nonstick frying pan on medium heat. Add the egg mixture and cook, stirring gently, until it starts to set, then sprinkle with mushrooms and cheese. Fold the omelette in half.

TO SERVE: Place omelette on a warmed platter for guests to help themselves.

MUSHROOMS

2 Tbsp butter

2 cups mixed mushrooms
(oyster, shimeji, chanterelle)

1 shallot, chopped

1 Tbsp chopped parsley

1 Tbsp chopped chives

OMELETTE

12 eggs

⅓ cup whipping cream

2 Tbsp butter

⅓ cup grated chèvre noir

BRIOCHE FRENCH TOAST

WITH BOURBON MAPLE SYRUP,

SOUR CREAM MOUSSE AND CANDIED PECANS

CANDIED PECANS

2 cups pecan halves

4 Tbsp simple syrup (page 137)

PASTRY CREAM

1 cup milk

⅔ cup sugar

1 egg

⅓ cup cornstarch

MOUSSE

3 sheets gelatin

½ cup pastry cream

¾ cup sour cream

2 cups whipping cream

¼ cup sugar

MAPLE SYRUP

¾ oz bourbon
(your favourite brand)

1 cup maple syrup

FRENCH TOAST

4 eggs

1 cup milk

⅓ cup whipping cream

½ tsp vanilla extract

1 tsp sugar

1 tsp ground cinnamon

½ vanilla bean, pulp only

8 slices brioche, 1-inch thick

4 Tbsp unsalted butter

Icing sugar, for garnish

WHAT MAKES this French toast so sumptuous is using brioche instead of bread. Thanks to the high butter content of brioche, it just melts in your mouth. We make our own brioche, but you can buy it from your favourite bakery. The bourbon maple syrup, sour cream mousse and candied pecans make this a brunch dish fit for kings and queens.

To get the pulp from the vanilla bean, slice it in half lengthwise. Use the back of the knife to scrape the pulp out of the pod. *Serves 4*

CANDIED PECANS: Preheat the oven to 325°F. Toss pecans in simple syrup, then spread out on a parchment-lined baking sheet. Bake in the oven, stirring occasionally, for about 20 minutes, or until sugar on pecans is dry. Remove and allow to cool. Will keep in an airtight container for 2 to 3 weeks.

PASTRY CREAM: Combine milk and sugar in a small saucepan. Bring to a boil on medium heat, then remove from the stove.

Whisk together egg and cornstarch in a bowl, until well combined. Temper the egg mixture (so that it doesn't curdle) by whisking in 1 Tbsp of the hot milk mixture. Do this twice more. Add the remaining hot milk mixture and whisk well.

Return the milk and egg mixture to the saucepan on medium heat and cook, stirring well, for 2 to 3 minutes, or until thick. Remove from the stove.

MOUSSE: Soak gelatin leaves in a bowl of cold water for 1 to 2 minutes, or until softened. Take out gelatin leaves and squeeze out any excess liquid, then place them in a stainless steel bowl sitting on a small saucepan of boiling water on medium heat. Whisk in pastry cream. Remove from the stove and stir in sour cream, mixing well.

In a chilled bowl, whisk together whipping cream and sugar until soft peaks form. Fold into the gelatin mixture. Cover and refrigerate until needed.

MAPLE SYRUP: Mix together bourbon and maple syrup in a bowl. Adjust the amount of bourbon to suit your taste.

FRENCH TOAST: Preheat the oven to 450°F. Whisk together eggs, milk, cream, vanilla extract, sugar and cinnamon in a bowl. Transfer to a blender and purée. Strain through a fine-mesh sieve. Add vanilla pulp to the egg mixture and whisk well.

Transfer the egg mixture to a flat-bottomed dish and add brioche slices to soak for 5 minutes on each side.

Melt butter in two large ovenproof frying pans on medium heat. Add brioche slices and cook for about 10 minutes, or until golden. Turn over brioche slices, then place the frying pans in the oven for 3 to 4 minutes, or until nice and golden.

TO SERVE: Place two brioche slices on each of four warmed plates. Drizzle with bourbon maple syrup, then garnish with candied pecans, sour cream mousse and a dusting of icing sugar.

SMOKED SALMON
AND LEEK FRITTATA

BRUNCH is a very popular meal at Feenie's, and brunch means eggs. Did you know that a frittata is the opposite of an omelette? An omelette is simple to make but hard to get perfect. A frittata is much easier to get right. However, like an omelette, the secret to making a good frittata is to make sure you have a good nonstick frying pan. This is also a good dish for lunch or a light dinner or, as in Spain, a tapas. *Serves 4 to 6*

Preheat the oven to 350°F. Melt butter in a nonstick ovenproof frying pan on medium heat. Add leek and sauté for about 4 minutes, or until tender. Leave on the heat while you quickly prepare eggs.

Whisk together eggs and dill in a bowl. Gently fold in cream cheese, then pour over leek in the frying pan. Season with salt and freshly ground black pepper. Decrease the heat to medium-low and cook for about 4 minutes, or until the edges are set but the centre is still runny. Place the frying pan in the oven and bake the frittata for about 15 minutes, or until golden brown.

TO SERVE: Transfer the frittata to a warmed platter and cut into four or six wedges. Scatter smoked salmon strips over it. Garnish with mesclun.

1 Tbsp butter

1 medium leek, white and light green parts only, ¼-inch dice

8 large eggs

1 Tbsp chopped fresh dill

2 Tbsp cream cheese, in pea-size pieces

2 oz smoked salmon, cut in thin strips

mesclun (mixed salad greens), for garnish

CROQUE
MADAME

MORNAY SAUCE

2 Tbsp unsalted butter

2 Tbsp all-purpose flour

1½ cups milk, heated to boiling

Pinch of grated nutmeg

Pinch of cayenne pepper

½ cup grated
Emmental cheese

½ cup grated Gruyère cheese

CROQUE MADAME

4 slices sourdough
bread (each 1-inch thick)

3 Tbsp butter

8 slices ham

4 eggs

EVERYONE LOVES a grilled ham and cheese sandwich, so I decided to take it a step further by adding Mornay sauce with lots of cheese, then topping it off with a perfect fried egg. This is one of my favourites to eat on trips to France and at French bistros here in North America. *Serves 4*

MORNAY SAUCE: Melt butter in a heavy saucepan on low heat. Stirring constantly, add flour and cook slowly for about 2 minutes, until foamy or frothy but not brown. Remove from the stove, then vigorously whisk in heated milk until mixture is smooth. Stir in nutmeg and cayenne. Increase the heat to medium-high, then return sauce to the stove and boil for about 1 minute. Remove from the stove and stir in Emmental and Gruyère until well incorporated.

CROQUE MADAME: Preheat the oven to 300°F. Place sourdough slices on a baking sheet and toast in the oven for about 8 minutes.

Use 2 Tbsp of the butter to butter the toasted bread, then place a slice on each of four warmed plates. Drizzle 2 Tbsp of the Mornay sauce over each slice of toast, then top each with 2 slices of ham.

Melt the remaining butter in a frying pan on medium heat. Add eggs and fry for about 4 minutes, or until whites are no longer transparent.

TO SERVE: Place a fried egg on top of each open-faced sandwich and drizzle with more Mornay sauce to taste.

SCRAMBLED EGGS
WITH SPINACH AND
RÖSTI POTATO

PANCETTA CRISP
4 thin slices pancetta

POTATOES
2 large Yukon Gold potatoes
½ cup rendered
duck fat (page 135)

SPINACH
2 Tbsp butter
4 handfuls of spinach
½ shallot, chopped
¼ cup whipping cream

SCRAMBLED EGGS
8 eggs
2 Tbsp butter

ONE OF MY first cooking jobs was with Rolf Gunther at the Rim Rock Café, where the most popular brunch dish was rösti potato with poached eggs and smoked salmon. At Feenie's, we make a thicker rösti so that it is moist in the centre, and instead of the poached eggs, we top it with scrambled eggs. And instead of smoked salmon, we use spinach and pancetta. Truly delicious. *Serves 4*

PANCETTA CRISP: Preheat the oven to 325°F. Place pancetta between 2 baking sheets lined with parchment paper, then bake in the oven for 10 to 15 minutes, or until nice and crispy. Remove from the oven.

POTATOES: Preheat the oven to 400°F. Coarsely grate potatoes and season with salt. Place in a clean tea towel and squeeze to remove excess water. Form grated potato into 4 round flat patties about 1-inch thick. Season with salt and freshly ground white pepper.

Melt duck fat in an ovenproof frying pan on medium heat. Add potato patties and sear for 4 minutes on each side. Place the frying pan in the oven and bake the rösti for about 10 minutes, or until golden brown. Remove from the oven and keep warm.

SPINACH: While the rösti are cooking, melt butter in a frying pan on high heat. Add spinach and shallot, then sauté for about 10 minutes, or until the water from the spinach is all gone. Add cream and cook for about 5 minutes, or until reduced by half.

SCRAMBLED EGGS: Place the eggs in a bowl and whisk. Heat butter in a nonstick frying pan on high heat. Add eggs and cook, stirring occasionally, for about 4 minutes, until soft curds form.

TO SERVE: Place a rösti on each of four warmed plates and top with spinach, then scrambled eggs. Garnish each with a crispy pancetta slice.

LEEK AND GOAT CHEESE PHYLLO TART

A TASTY APPETIZER sets the tone for a good dinner, and this tart is an excellent starter. It's also perfect for brunch or a light lunch when paired with a side salad. The most important thing to keep in mind when you use phyllo is that it dries out quickly, so work fast! *Serves 4 as brunch or lunch, 8 as an appetizer*

Preheat the oven to 350°F. Heat oil in a large frying pan on medium-high heat. Add leeks and sauté for about 5 minutes, or until softened. Remove from the stove, then season with salt and freshly ground white pepper.

Mix together goat cheese and ricotta in a bowl. Whisk in parsley, dill, chives and eggs until well incorporated. Season with salt and freshly ground white pepper. Add the leek mixture and stir in well.

Brush an 8-inch diameter pie plate with some of the melted butter. Brush 1 phyllo sheet with melted butter and place over the pie plate. Butter a second sheet and place it over the first sheet at an angle, so that about 3 inches of one corner of the first sheet is not covered. Continue to brush with melted butter and overlap the phyllo sheets in a circular form, until you've used them all. Press phyllo down lightly to take the shape of the pie plate.

Add the leek and cheese filling, leaving a 1-inch border free around the edge of the phyllo. Fold the overhanging phyllo over the filling, then make a free-form "crimped" edge. Brush melted butter along the edge.

Place in the oven on the bottom shelf and bake for 20 to 25 minutes, or until the pastry is golden and the filling is set.

TO SERVE: Cut into wedges and place on four or eight individual warmed plates. Serve warm or at room temperature.

2 Tbsp olive oil

6 cups sliced leeks, white and light green parts only

½ cup goat cheese

1½ cups ricotta cheese

3 Tbsp chopped fresh parsley

3 Tbsp chopped fresh dill

3 Tbsp chopped fresh chives

3 eggs, beaten

⅓ cup melted butter

10 sheets frozen phyllo, thawed

SPINACH, PROSCIUTTO AND PEACH SALAD

I LOVE WARM FRUIT with greens, and this salad is a perfect blend of sweet peaches, crisp greens and tart goat cheese. When fresh summer peaches are not available, use fresh figs. The dressing for this salad is quite simple—just olive oil and lemon juice—because the wonderful butter and balsamic mixture on the peaches gives the salad its main flavour. This is a perfect brunch, lunch or light dinner in the summer. *Serves 4*

DRESSING: Whisk together oil and lemon in a bowl. Season with salt and freshly ground white pepper.

PEACHES: Cut peach into 8 wedges. Place balsamic vinegar and honey in a saucepan on medium heat, bring to a boil and cook for about 5 minutes, until reduced by half. Add butter and mix well. Add peach wedges, toss lightly to coat, then sauté for 1 to 2 minutes. (You are not cooking the peach wedges, just simply warming them.) Remove from the stove.

SALAD: Toss together spinach and dressing in a large bowl. Season with salt and freshly ground white pepper.

TO SERVE: Divide spinach among four large salad plates or bowls. Top each serving with 2 peach wedges, then drizzle with the butter-balsamic mixture from the frying pan. Place 2 slices of prosciutto on each salad and sprinkle with goat cheese.

DRESSING

⅝ cup extra-virgin olive oil

¼ lemon, juice only

PEACHES

1 large ripe peach,
peeled and pitted

½ cup balsamic vinegar

1 Tbsp honey

1 Tbsp unsalted butter

SALAD

1 large bunch spinach,
destemmed

8 slices prosciutto

1 cup goat cheese, crumbled

HOMEMADE GRANOLA

LAVENDER HONEY

¼ cup honey

1 Tbsp dried organic lavender

GRANOLA

2 cups quick-cooking oats

¼ cup shredded coconut

¼ cup slivered almonds

¼ cup chopped cashews

2 Tbsp poppy seeds

¼ cup sunflower seeds

2 Tbsp sesame seeds

¼ cup dark brown sugar

½ tsp vanilla extract

¼ cup golden raisins

¼ cup dark raisins

OUTSIDE OF A SMOOTHIE for breakfast, another of my favourites is granola with organic fruit and yogurt. Here is my recipe for homemade granola—the honey infused with the lavender adds a nice note. Just drizzle it on before serving. *Serves 6 to 8*

LAVENDER HONEY: Place honey and lavender in a small saucepan on medium heat for 2 minutes. Strain through a fine-mesh sieve and discard lavender. Allow honey to cool. Store in a covered container, will keep for months.

GRANOLA: Preheat the oven to 350°F. Place 7 pieces of aluminum foil on a large baking sheet. Place oats, coconut, almonds, cashews, poppy seeds, sunflower seeds and sesame seeds onto separate pieces of foil; spread out evenly in a thin layer. Bake in the oven for 5 to 8 minutes, or until golden brown and toasted. Each ingredient will take a different time, so keep an eye on them and remove each one from the oven as soon as it is done.

Place warm oats in a bowl, then stir in brown sugar and vanilla. Add coconut, almonds and cashews, then toss together gently. Add poppy, sunflower and sesame seeds. Add golden and dark raisins. Toss gently. Allow to cool. Will keep in an airtight container for 2 months.

TO SERVE: Place some granola in each bowl. Add a layer of plain yogurt and drizzle with lavender honey.

SMOOTHIES

SMOOTHIES ARE SOMETHING I enjoy making and drinking at home. When you're in a hurry and you need a breakfast that is delicious, nutritious and fast, try one of these tasty combinations. And remember that smoothies are best served ice-cold. These recipes require a large blender that will hold 2 to 3 quarts, but you can make the smoothies in two or three batches in a smaller blender, then combine the batches in a large bowl before serving. *Each recipe serves 4*

Put juice (and coconut milk) in the blender first, then add yogurt, fruit and honey. Blend at high speed until smooth. Pour into four 16-oz glasses and add straws.

TROPICAL SMOOTHIE

¼ cup coconut milk

¼ cup passion fruit juice

1½ cups pineapple juice

1 cup plain yogurt

½ banana

2 cups fresh pineapple chunks

1 cup mango, peeled, pitted and diced

1 cup papaya, peeled, deseeded and diced

4 Tbsp honey (or to taste)

STRAWBERRY-KIWI SMOOTHIE

2 cups apple juice

1 cup plain yogurt

1 cup peaches, peeled, pitted and diced

1½ cups strawberries, hulled

1½ cups kiwis, peeled and diced

2 Tbsp honey (or to taste)

CHERRY AND BERRIES SMOOTHIE

1 cup cranberry juice

1 cup apple juice

1½ cups plain yogurt

1½ cups cherries, pitted

1½ cups strawberries, hulled

½ cup cranberries

½ cup raspberries

4 Tbsp honey (or to taste)

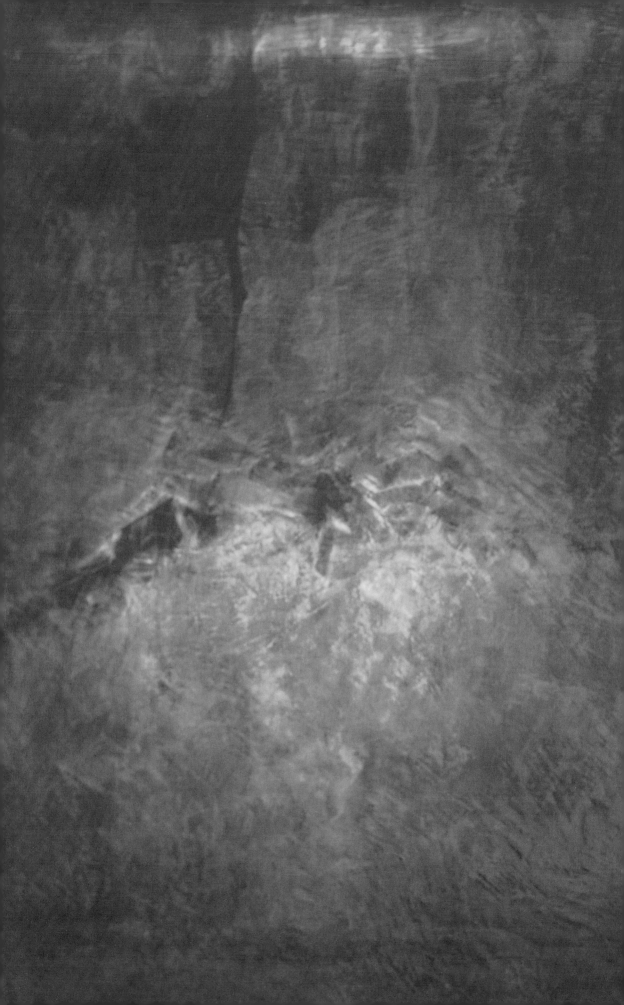

FEENIE'S LUNCH

GRILLED SPICY CALAMARI
AND GREEN BEAN SALAD

¾ cup nuoc cham

1 cup water

½ stalk lemon grass,
crushed and chopped

1 clove garlic, roughly chopped

3 Thai chilies,
deseeded and chopped

1 cup palm sugar
(Asian food stores)

POTATOES

4 baby Yukon Gold potatoes

¾ cup nuoc cham dressing

½ tsp Dijon mustard

VINAIGRETTE

⅓ cup nuoc cham dressing

1½ tsp Dijon mustard

2 Tbsp fresh lime juice

½ cup extra-virgin olive oil

¼ cup sunflower oil

SALAD

1 cup green beans, trimmed,
cut into 1½-inch lengths

5 to 10 calamari tubes,
pointy ends trimmed off

½ tsp extra-virgin olive oil

1 cup tomato concassé
(page 137)

2 tsp fresh lime juice

1 Tbsp chopped fresh Thai basil

1 Tbsp chopped fresh tarragon

1 Tbsp chopped fresh parsley

½ cup nuoc cham vinaigrette

Cilantro oil (page 137),
for garnish

WE OFFER THIS SALAD at Feenie's because I love grilled calamari. This recipe is not complicated, it just has several steps. Nuoc cham is a Vietnamese fish sauce that is sold in most Asian markets and is key to the flavour of the dish. Thai chilies, also called red or bird's eye chilies, can be found in Asian markets. *Serves 2 to 4*

DRESSING: Combine all the ingredients in a small saucepan on high heat. Bring to a boil and cook for about 5 minutes, or until reduced by half. Remove from the stove and allow to cool. Cover and refrigerate for 24 hours to allow the flavours to ripen. Strain through a fine-mesh sieve before using. Will keep in the refrigerator for 2 weeks.

POTATOES: Thinly slice potatoes. Bring a saucepan filled with salted water to a boil on high heat. Add potatoes and cook for about 8 minutes, just until no longer crunchy. Drain and place potatoes in a microwave-safe dish.

Combine nuoc cham dressing and mustard in a small bowl. Pour over potatoes. Cook on high for 30 seconds in a microwave.

VINAIGRETTE: Combine nuoc cham dressing, mustard and lime juice in a bowl. Slowly whisk in olive oil and sunflower oil. Season with salt and freshly ground white pepper.

SALAD: Fill a bowl with ice water. Bring a saucepan of salted water to a boil. Place green beans in the boiling water and cook for 3 minutes. Take out green beans and immediately put them into the ice water to stop the cooking. When green beans are cool, take them out of the ice water and drain on paper towels.

Preheat the grill on high heat. Slit open each calamari tube lengthwise down one side, then spread them out flat on a clean surface. Season with salt and freshly ground white pepper. Sprinkle with just a touch of the oil. Grill calamari for just 1½ minutes on each side (be sure not to overcook), then remove from the heat. Slice lengthwise into strips. Do not worry when the strips curl up.

Place calamari in a large bowl. Add green beans, tomato concassé, lime juice, Thai basil, tarragon, parsley and nuoc cham vinaigrette. Toss together well.

TO SERVE: Arrange potato slices in a circle on each of two (or four) plates. Mound warm salad on top of the potatoes. Garnish with cilantro oil.

GRILLED QUAIL AND BRAISED ENDIVE SALAD

VINAIGRETTE

½ cup blood orange juice

2 Tbsp sherry vinegar

1½ tsp honey

Pinch of grated fresh ginger

1 cup extra-virgin olive oil

COMPOUND BUTTER

¼ cup unsalted butter, softened

1 Tbsp fresh lemon juice

1 tsp chopped fresh parsley

½ tsp chopped garlic

ENDIVE

4 endives, cut in half

2 tsp liquid honey

½ lemon, juice only

2 Tbsp canola oil

⅓ cup dry white wine

2 cups dark chicken stock, heated (page 132)

SALAD

1 cup tawny port

4 quails, deboned

8 cups mesclun (mixed salad greens)

4 Tbsp fried sliced shallots

FOR THIS RECIPE, you can either grill the quail on the barbecue or panfry them. You can use regular oranges, but try to get blood oranges (they're in season from mid-January to early April). Fried sliced shallots are sold in specialty stores. This dish makes an excellent light lunch or appetizer before dinner. *Serves 4*

VINAIGRETTE: Combine orange juice, vinegar, honey and ginger in a small bowl. Slowly whisk in oil. Season with salt and freshly ground white pepper.

COMPOUND BUTTER: Combine butter, lemon juice, parsley, garlic, salt and freshly ground white pepper in a bowl. Mix well until ingredients are evenly distributed. Place the mixture on a piece of plastic wrap or parchment paper, then roll into a cylinder about 1½ inches in diameter. Twist the ends of the parchment. Refrigerate until needed.

ENDIVE: Preheat the oven to 375°F. Toss endives with honey and lemon juice in a bowl. Season with salt and white pepper.

Heat oil in a large frying pan on medium-high heat. Add endive and sear for 2 minutes on each side, or until browned. Add wine and stir to deglaze the bottom of the pan. Transfer endive and cooking juices to a shallow ovenproof dish. Add hot stock to cover endive. Cover the dish with aluminum foil. Place in the oven and cook for 10 to 12 minutes, or until endive is softened. Remove from the oven.

SALAD: Place port in a saucepan on low heat and simmer for about 10 minutes, or until reduced to ⅓ cup.

Preheat the barbecue on high heat. Grill quails for 3 to 5 minutes, or until cooked through (juices should run clear when you insert a knife into the leg joint). Transfer quails to a warmed platter, top each with a slice of the compound butter and keep in a warm spot.

TO SERVE: Toss mesclun with dressing in a bowl, then divide among four plates. Top each salad with 2 pieces of warm endive and a quail. Garnish with fried shallots and a drizzle of reduced port.

HALIBUT

WHAT MAKES THIS DISH special is the smokiness of the bacon, the sharpness of the sherry vinegar and the sweetness of the brown sugar. When I think about treating seafood delicately and simply, I immediately think of Eric Ripert at Le Bernardin in New York and Hidekazu Tojo at Tojo's in Vancouver. Like them, I prefer to present fish without too many garnishes, so I suggest that you serve any vegetables on the side. *Serves 4*

VINAIGRETTE: Sauté bacon in a frying pan on medium heat for about 3 minutes, or until crisp but not burned. Add garlic and shallot, then cook for 1 minute. Add vinegar and stir to deglaze the bottom of the pan. Stir in sugar. Remove from the stove, then slowly whisk in oil. Season with salt and freshly ground white pepper.

HALIBUT: Preheat the oven to 400°F. Season halibut with salt and freshly ground white pepper. Heat oil in an ovenproof frying pan on high heat. Add halibut and sear on one side for 3 to 5 minutes, or until browned. Turn halibut over, then place the frying pan in the oven and cook for 4 to 6 minutes, or until done (flesh is opaque and flakes easily with a fork).

TO SERVE: Place a piece of halibut on each of four warmed plates and drizzle with bacon vinaigrette.

VINAIGRETTE

¼ cup chopped bacon

1 small clove garlic, minced

1 small shallot, chopped

¼ cup sherry vinegar

2 tsp brown sugar

¼ cup extra-virgin olive oil

HALIBUT

4 pieces halibut (each 6 oz)

3 Tbsp olive oil

DUCK CONFIT SALAD

WHAT MAKES THIS RECIPE special is the spice rub for the duck legs and the marinating. The great thing is that you can make the duck confit a long time ahead. In this dish, the richness of the duck and Gorgonzola are offset by the acidity of the hazelnut vinaigrette. *Serves 6*

SPICE RUB: Use a coffee grinder or spice mill to grind all the spices and dried herbs to a fine powder. Mix all the ground ingredients together well.

DUCK CONFIT: Dip the flesh side of the duck legs into the spice rub and place them in a single layer, skin side up, in a shallow baking pan. Refrigerate uncovered for 18 to 24 hours.

Preheat the oven to 325°F. Rinse duck under cold running water to remove the spice rub. Place duck legs in a single layer, skin side up, in a non-aluminum roasting pan, then add rosemary, thyme, sage and garlic.

Melt duck fat in a saucepan on medium heat and pour over duck legs, covering them completely. Cover the roasting pan with aluminum foil. Bake in the oven for 2 to 3 hours, or until the meat falls off the bone. Remove from the oven and allow duck to cool in the fat. Strain duck fat through a fine-mesh sieve. Place duck legs in an airtight container and cover with strained duck fat. The duck confit can be prepared ahead up to this point; will keep in the refrigerator for up to 1 month or in the freezer for up to 1 year.

BACON-HAZELNUT VINAIGRETTE: Sauté bacon in a frying pan on low heat for about 15 minutes, or until crisp but not burned. Remove from the heat. Take bacon out of the pan and set aside. Pour out and discard bacon fat except for 2 Tbsp.

Return the frying pan with the reserved bacon fat to the stove on medium heat. Add garlic and shallots, then sauté for 3 to 5 minutes, or until translucent. Stir in brown sugar. Add vinegar and stir to deglaze the bottom of the pan. Stir in mustard. Remove from the stove and allow to cool. Slowly whisk in olive oil, hazelnut oil and crispy bacon.

recipe continued overleaf >

SPICE RUB

2 Tbsp fine sea salt

2 Tbsp dried thyme leaves

2 Tbsp dried rosemary leaves

1½ Tbsp black peppercorns

1 Tbsp star anise

1 Tbsp fennel seeds

1 Tbsp ground cinnamon

1 Tbsp cloves

2 tsp coriander seeds

1 tsp Szechuan peppercorns

DUCK CONFIT

6 large duck legs, trimmed of excess fat

2 sprigs fresh rosemary

3 sprigs fresh thyme

1 sprig fresh sage

1 bulb garlic, cut in half horizontally

2 quarts rendered duck fat (page 135)

BACON-HAZELNUT VINAIGRETTE

3½ oz bacon, finely diced

2 cloves garlic, minced

2 shallots, finely chopped

2 Tbsp brown sugar

½ cup red wine vinegar

2 tsp Dijon mustard

½ cup extra-virgin olive oil

½ cup hazelnut oil

1 Tbsp Dijon mustard

½ cup apple cider vinegar

⅔ cup sunflower oil

⅔ cup hazelnut oil

SALAD

2 heads butter lettuce

1 head radicchio

2 bunches arugula

1½ cups thumbnail-sized
chunks of Gorgonzola cheese

HAZELNUT VINAIGRETTE: Whisk together mustard and vinegar in a bowl. Slowly whisk in sunflower oil and hazelnut oil. Season with salt and freshly ground white pepper.

FINISH DUCK CONFIT: Preheat the oven to 400°F. Remove duck legs from fat and wipe off excess with a paper towel. Heat a large, heavy, ovenproof frying pan on medium-high heat, then add duck, skin side down. When you see the fat starting to melt out of the duck and the skin starting to turn brown, place the frying pan in the oven. (Do not try to move the legs and do not turn them over.) Sear in the oven for 6 to 7 minutes, or until duck is heated through. Remove from the oven, then carefully take duck legs out of the pan and drain on paper towels.

SALAD: Toss together lettuce, radicchio, arugula and hazelnut vinaigrette in a large bowl.

TO SERVE: Divide salad among six plates and sprinkle with Gorgonzola. Place a duck leg, skin side up, on top of each serving. Warm the bacon-hazelnut vinaigrette in the microwave on high heat for 30 seconds, then drizzle over the duck.

CHICKEN THIGHS IN WHITE WINE

WITH BUTTER-BRAISED TOMATOES

WHEN IT COMES to chicken, I am a leg and thigh man because of the richer flavour of the darker meat. This dish makes delicious leftovers, so you might want to make a double batch and save half for later. Serve the chicken with mashed potatoes and steamed green beans. The butter-braised tomatoes also make a tasty accompaniment for a breakfast, pasta or cheese dish. *Serves 4*

BUTTER-BRAISED TOMATOES: Preheat the oven to 150°F. Place tomatoes on a baking sheet. Sprinkle with thyme, rosemary, butter, salt and freshly ground white pepper. Place in the oven and cook slowly for 3 hours. Remove from the oven and allow to cool. Will keep in the refrigerator for 2 days.

CHICKEN: Preheat the oven to 400°F. Toss carrot, onion and celery and 3 Tbsp of the oil in a roasting pan (just big enough to hold the chicken later), then roast in the oven for 20 to 25 minutes, or until browned. Remove from the oven and decrease the heat to 325°F.

Season chicken with salt and freshly ground white pepper. Heat the remaining oil in a frying pan on medium-high heat. Add chicken, skin side down, and sear for 3 to 5 minutes on each side, or until skin is well browned. Transfer to paper towels and drain.

Combine wine and stock in a saucepan on high heat and bring to a boil. Season lightly with salt. Remove from the stove.

Arrange chicken thighs close together on top of the vegetables in the roasting pan. Cover with the heated wine mixture. Sprinkle with sage, rosemary, thyme, garlic and peppercorns. Cover the pan with aluminum foil and cook in the oven for 1 hour, or until meat is nearly falling off the bone. Carefully remove chicken pieces from the sauce and keep warm.

Strain sauce through a fine-mesh sieve into a saucepan. Cook on high heat for 10 to 20 minutes, or until reduced to 1 cup.

TO SERVE: Reheat butter-braised tomatoes and place on four warmed plates. Top each serving with 2 pieces of chicken, then drizzle with the reduced sauce.

BUTTER-BRAISED
TOMATOES

10 Roma tomatoes, cut in half

1 tsp thyme

1 tsp rosemary

¼ cup unsalted butter,
1-inch cubes

CHICKEN

1 carrot, ½-inch dice

1 onion, ½-inch dice

2 stalks celery, ½-inch dice

½ cup canola oil

8 chicken thighs

2 cups white dry wine

2 quarts dark chicken
stock (page 132)

1 sprig fresh sage

1 sprig fresh rosemary

1 sprig fresh thyme

5 cloves garlic

8 black peppercorns

THE FEENIE
BURGER

RELISH

1¾ lbs pickling cucumbers, roughly chopped

1 tsp mustard seeds

¼ tsp turmeric

¼ tsp celery seeds

1 Thai chili, deseeded and roughly chopped (page 24)

1 clove garlic, chopped

⅔ cup cider vinegar

½ cup sugar

2 tsp salt

1 cup finely chopped onion

⅔ cup finely chopped red bell pepper

2 bay leaves

ONIONS

4 Tbsp canola oil

4 onions, sliced

HAMBURGERS

5 lbs ground chuck

¾ cup finely diced red onion

¼ cup chopped Italian (flat-leaf) parsley

¼ cup chopped fresh chives

2 Tbsp sambal oelek (Indonesian chili-garlic sauce)

2 Tbsp Worcestershire sauce

1 Tbsp minced garlic

2 to 4 Tbsp canola or sunflower oil

8 to 12 slices cheddar cheese

8 to 12 hamburger buns, cut in half

Slices of tomato, to taste

Leaves of lettuce, to taste

1 cup sautéed button mushrooms

Slices of dill pickle, to taste

WHEN WE were creating our burger at Feenie's, we experimented with different mixtures of meat and different grinds. The simplest was the best. We use fresh-ground chuck that is 7 to 8 per cent fat. What's really important is to use a medium grind. Get your butcher to grind the meat for you, then cook these hamburgers the same day. For a truly decadent version, Feenie's offers a garnish of short-rib meat and/or pan-seared foie gras. *Makes 8 to 12 patties*

RELISH: Place pickling cucumbers, mustard seeds, turmeric, celery seeds, chili, garlic, vinegar, sugar and salt in a food processor and chop finely. Transfer the mixture to a large saucepan. Add onion, red bell pepper and bay leaves. Cook on medium-low heat for about 1 hour, stirring occasionally, until liquid is reduced. Remove from the stove and allow to cool. Refrigerate until ready to use. Makes about 2 cups. Will keep in the refrigerator for 1 month.

ONIONS: Heat oil in a large frying pan on medium to medium-high heat. Add onions and cook for 10 to 15 minutes, stirring and scraping the bottom of the pan, until evenly caramelized. When the onions are dark brown, remove from the stove. May be made ahead and refrigerated until needed.

HAMBURGERS: Combine ground beef, red onion, parsley, chives, sambal oelek, Worcestershire sauce, garlic, salt and pepper in a large bowl. Mix well until ingredients are evenly distributed. Divide into 8 to 12 portions and form each into a patty about ½-inch thick. Cover and refrigerate until needed.

Lightly oil the grill and preheat the barbecue to high heat. Grill patties until desired doneness (7 to 8 minutes for medium-rare, 12 to 15 minutes for well done), topping each patty with a slice of cheese for the last 2 minutes.

TO SERVE: Place each patty on the bottom half of a hamburger bun. Garnish with relish, caramelized onions, tomato, lettuce, mushrooms and dill pickle. Top with the other half of each bun.

also shown, in background:

THE FEENIE WEENIE

THE FEENIE
WEENIE

SPICE SACHET

1 star anise

½ tsp coriander

½ tsp black peppercorns

½ tsp mustard seeds

1 clove garlic

½ cinnamon stick

1 bay leaf

1 juniper berry

CHOUCROUTE

4 oz bacon, cut into small chunks

1½ cups sliced onions

2 cups good-quality sauerkraut

1⅓ cups Riesling

WEENIES

4 good-quality cheese smokies

2 cups choucroute

4 hot dog buns, cut in half

HAVING A LAST NAME like Feenie has not been easy. People always make the notorious weenie comment, but after a session joking around before we opened Feenie's, everyone agreed that the hot dog had to be called the "Feenie Weenie." Our friends at Oyama Sausage make one of the finest cheese smokies anywhere, and our friends at Terra Breads make an impeccable hot dog bun! I love weenies with sauerkraut, and we serve ours with choucroute (the French version of sauerkraut), but you can also serve it without. It's also good with charcuteries (page 106) or pork chops. *Serves 4*

SPICE SACHET: Place all the ingredients on a 6-inch square of cheesecloth and tie closed with kitchen string.

CHOUCROUTE: Cook bacon in a frying pan on medium heat for 10 to 15 minutes, or until crispy. Add onion and sauté for 5 to 7 minutes, or until translucent. Add sauerkraut, Riesling and spice sachet, then cook for about 45 minutes, or until liquid is reduced by two-thirds. Remove from the stove and allow to cool. Refrigerate for 24 hours for the flavours to develop. Makes 1 quart. Will keep in the refrigerator for up to 1 month.

WEENIES: Preheat the barbecue to high heat. Bring a saucepan of water to simmer on medium-high heat, then drop in smokies and cook for 5 minutes. Take out smokies and grill them for 5 to 7 minutes, or until plumped up and starting to ooze cheese.

TO SERVE: While weenies are grilling, heat up choucroute and toast hot dog buns. Place a layer of choucroute in each bun and add a smokie.

FEENIE'S
VEGGIE BURGER

THE CURRY MAYONNAISE is versatile. You can use it to perk up so many dishes. I use it on calamari sandwiches on sourdough bread (that recipe is in one of my earlier cookbooks, *Lumière Light,* but back then I used tartar sauce in the sandwich). I also love the curry mayonnaise as a dipping sauce for french fries. *Makes 10 to 12 patties*

CURRY MAYONNAISE: Place sun-dried tomatoes in a bowl and cover with boiling water. Let sit for 15 minutes, then drain and chop finely. Mix together sun-dried tomatoes, mayonnaise, cilantro, curry powder and lime juice until ingredients are evenly distributed and the colour is consistent. Cover and refrigerate until needed. Makes about 1¼ cups. Will keep in the refrigerator for 1 week.

VEGGIE BURGERS: Place one of the cans of drained garbanzo beans in a food processor and process until coarse but not puréed. Transfer to a large bowl.

Place the other can of drained garbanzo beans, lime juice, egg, minced and roasted garlic, ginger, ground cumin and ground coriander in a food processor, then process until smooth. Add this to the coarse bean mixture. Add cilantro, shallots, red and yellow bell peppers, jalapeño, mushrooms, pumpkins seeds, corn and panko. If the mixture feels a little damp, add more panko. It should be dry and crumbly (it will stay put when pressed together later).

Divide the mixture into 10 to 12 portions and form each into a patty ½- to ¾-inch thick. Heat 2 Tbsp of the oil in a large frying pan on medium-high heat. Add patties and fry (adding more oil as needed) in batches of two or three for 4 to 5 minutes on each side, or until golden brown.

TO SERVE: Place each patty on the bottom half of a hamburger bun. Garnish with a dollop of curry mayonnaise, tomatoes, onions and sprouts. Top with the other half of each bun.

CURRY MAYONNAISE

2 sun-dried tomatoes

1 cup mayonnaise (page 136)

¼ bunch cilantro, finely chopped

1½ Tbsp Madras curry powder

1 lime, juice only

VEGGIE BURGERS

2 cans (each 28 oz) garbanzo beans or chickpeas, drained

½ cup fresh lime juice

1 egg

1 clove garlic, minced

2 cloves garlic, roasted and chopped

1 Tbsp minced fresh ginger

½ Tbsp ground cumin

½ Tbsp ground coriander

½ bunch fresh cilantro, finely chopped

½ cup minced shallots

½ cup finely chopped red bell pepper

½ cup finely chopped yellow bell pepper

½ jalapeño pepper, deseeded and finely chopped

1 cup cooked sliced mushrooms

½ cup shelled raw pumpkin seeds

½ cup corn kernels

1 cup or more panko (Japanese bread crumbs)

½ cup canola oil

10 to 12 sesame seed hamburger buns, cut in half

Sliced tomatoes, to taste

Sliced onions, to taste

Sunflower sprouts, to taste

AHI TUNA SANDWICH

THIS SANDWICH combines the richness of guacamole with the unusual flavour of shiso. Shiso is a Japanese herb that is occasionally used in sushi and tempura. Although shiso can be found in most specialty Japanese stores, you may substitute cilantro if you wish. Be sure to get a very good-quality cut of tuna. *Serves 4*

SHISO GUACAMOLE: Mash avocados with lime juice and sour cream in a bowl. Stir in garlic, red onion, jalapeño and shiso. Season to taste with salt. Cover and refrigerate until needed.

SANDWICH: Combine oil and lemon zest in a bowl. Add tuna, cover and marinate for at least 20 minutes in the refrigerator.

Preheat the grill to high heat. Remove tuna from the marinade and pat dry with paper towels, then season with salt and freshly ground white pepper. Grill for only 1 minute, then turn over and grill for only 1 minute (be careful not to overcook).

TO SERVE: Place tomatoes, onions and butter lettuce on the bottom half of each bun. Top with a piece of tuna, a dollop of guacamole and the other half of each bun.

SHISO GUACAMOLE

2 ripe avocados, pitted and peeled

1 lime, juice only

¼ cup sour cream

1 large clove garlic, minced

½ small red onion, finely diced

½ jalapeño pepper, deseeded and finely diced

4 shiso leaves, thinly sliced

SANDWICH

1½ cups olive oil

2 lemons, zest only

4 pieces ahi tuna loin (each 3 to 4 oz)

4 olive oil buns or Portuguese buns, cut in half

Sliced tomatoes, to taste

Sliced onions, to taste

Leaves of butter lettuce, to taste

CORN, CARAMELIZED ONION
AND CHANTERELLE RAVIOLI
WITH PEKING DUCK BROTH

Pasta dough with
semolina (page 138)

Peking duck broth (page 135)

FILLING

2 Tbsp olive oil

4½ onions, finely diced

2 ears peaches and cream
corn, kernels only

1¼ cups chanterelle
mushrooms

1 Tbsp vegetable oil

1 Tbsp butter

2 tsp minced shallots

5 cloves garlic, minced

¼ cup dry white wine

½ cup whipping cream

2 Tbsp fresh thyme leaves

ORN with caramelized onions and chanterelles is a magical combination. You can serve this ravioli with a cream or butter sauce, but I prefer to serve it with Peking duck broth. The best thing is that you can make this dish ahead of time. *Makes 40 ravioli*

FILLING: Heat olive oil in a saucepan on medium-high heat. Add onions and cook, stirring frequently, for 15 to 20 minutes, or until caramelized. Add corn and cook for 10 minutes. Remove from the stove.

Place chanterelles in a food processor and pulse until pieces are about the size of corn kernels. In a frying pan, heat vegetable oil and butter on medium heat. Add chanterelles and sauté for about 5 minutes, or until they start to get limp. Add shallots and garlic, then sauté for about 3 minutes. Season with salt and freshly ground white pepper. Add wine and stir to deglaze the bottom of the pan. Cook for 5 to 7 minutes, or until wine is reduced to nothing. Add cream and cook for 10 to 15 minutes, or until reduced by half.

Combine the chanterelle and onion mixtures. Add thyme, then season to taste with salt and freshly ground white pepper. Allow to cool, then cover and refrigerate until needed.

Stuff the ravioli according to the instructions with the pasta dough recipe.

Bring a stockpot of salted water to a boil on high heat. Cook frozen ravioli for about 4½ minutes (fresh ravioli for about 3 minutes), or until al dente. Drain in a colander.

TO SERVE: Divide ravioli among four warmed plates. Drizzle ¼ cup of Peking duck broth over each serving.

SPAGHETTINI

I'VE TRIED to choose recipes that are fun, not too hard to make and excitingly full of flavour. This happens to be all of the above. You can make this dish year-round if you use hot-house cherry tomatoes, but I think it is best in the summer, when cherry tomatoes are in season. *Serves 4*

Gently toss together cherry tomatoes, garlic, chili and oil in a large bowl.

Bring a stockpot of salted water to a boil. Add spaghettini and cook for 5 to 6 minutes, or until al dente. Drain in a colander, then add to the cherry tomato mixture.

TO SERVE: Add basil and Parmesan to pasta and toss gently but well. Divide among four warmed plates.

3 cups cherry
tomatoes, quartered

1 clove garlic, thinly sliced

1 Thai chili, deseeded and
finely chopped (page 24)

½ cup extra-virgin olive oil

1 lb dried spaghettini

¼ cup chopped fresh basil

¼ cup grated Parmesan

MOULES
ET FRITES

SPICY MAYONNAISE
1 cup mayonnaise (page 136)

Pinch of cayenne pepper

FRIES
3 quarts canola oil

2 lbs Yukon Gold potatoes

MUSSELS AND BROTH
4 Tbsp olive oil

2 Tbsp chopped lemon grass

2 Tbsp chopped ginger

1 Tbsp minced garlic

½ cup dry white wine

1 lb mussels, cleaned and debearded

1 cup shellfish stock (page 133)

½ red bell pepper, thinly sliced

½ yellow bell pepper, thinly sliced

½ leek, white part only, thinly sliced

1 Tbsp butter

1 lemon, juice only

Italian (flat-leaf) parsley, to taste

MOULES ET FRITES (mussels and fries) is one of the first dishes I had when I was fifteen on a trip to Belgium. Knowing nothing about food then, I accidentally ordered it and could not believe the gorgeous juiciness of the mussels, so it was inevitable that they would be on the Feenie's menu. We serve this dish with lots of good bread to mop up the juice. Dig in! *Serves 2*

SPICY MAYONNAISE: Combine mayonnaise and cayenne pepper in a bowl and mix well. Season with salt and freshly ground white pepper. Refrigerate until needed.

FRIES: Preheat the oil to 325°F in a deep fryer. Cut potatoes into fries ½ inch by 3 inches. In small batches, deep-fry potatoes for about 10 minutes, or until golden brown.

MUSSELS AND BROTH: Heat oil in a large saucepan on medium-high heat. Add lemon grass, ginger and garlic, then sauté for 1½ minutes, or until fragrant. Add wine and mussels, then cook for about 3 minutes until liquid is reduced by half.

Add stock, cover the pan with a lid, then cook on high heat for 1 to 3 minutes, or until mussel shells open. Take mussels out of the stock and set aside.

To the stock that the mussels were cooked in, add red and yellow bell peppers, leek, butter and lemon juice. Cook for about 5 minutes, or until vegetables are done. Season with salt and freshly ground white pepper.

TO SERVE: Divide mussels among two warmed bowls, then pour broth and vegetables over top. Garnish with parsley. Place fries on a warmed platter and serve a bowl of spicy mayonnaise on the side.

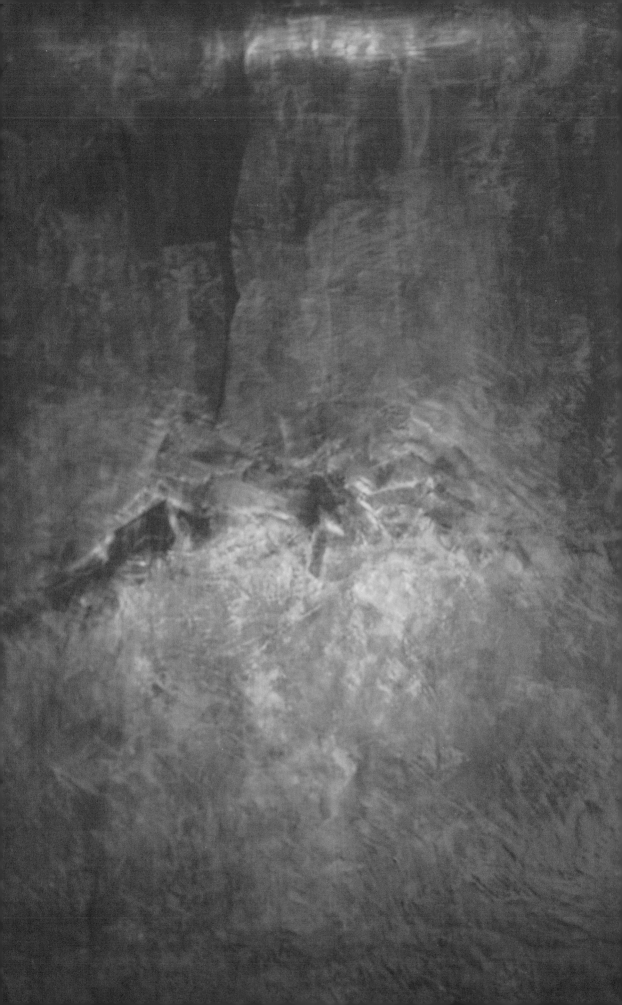

PAN-SEARED SALMON WITH GREEN PEA RISOTTO AND RED WINE SAUCE *44*

PAN-SEARED TROUT WITH CAULIFLOWER PURÉE AND POACHED OYSTERS *46*

SEARED SKATE WINGS WITH BROWN BUTTER SAUCE AND GREEN BEANS *47*

CRAB RAVIOLI WITH BLACK TRUFFLE BEURRE BLANC *49*

GRILLED LOBSTER WITH GARLIC BUTTER AND SAUCE VERTE *50*

CLAM AND PANCETTA SAUCE WITH LINGUINE *52*

BRAISED LAMB SHANK WITH RIGATONI *53*

ROAST CHICKEN WITH TOMATOES, ROASTED PEPPERS, OLIVES AND CAPERS *55*

HONEY-GLAZED DUCK WITH ORANGE GNOCCHI,
LEEK-FENNEL FONDANT AND ORANGE ROSEMARY JUS *56*

FEENIE'S DINNER

MAPLE-GLAZED PORK BELLY WITH NAVY BEAN PURÉE AND APPLE-BACON COMPOTE *59*

VEAL NEPTUNE WITH CRAB HOLLANDAISE AND MUSHROOM RAGOUT *62*

STEAK AND BLUE CHEESE PIE *64*

PAN-SEARED SALMON

SAUCE

2 cups Pinot Noir

4 sprigs fresh thyme

10 black peppercorns

1 shallot, roughly chopped

2 bay leaves

½ cup dark chicken
stock (page 132)

½ tsp honey

3 Tbsp unsalted butter

RISOTTO

3 to 4 cups chicken stock

6 Tbsp olive oil

4 large shallots, peeled
and finely chopped

2 cups arborio or carnaroli
rice, superfino quality

2 cups dry white wine

2 to 4 Tbsp freshly
grated Parmesan

3 Tbsp unsalted butter

4 Tbsp mascarpone cheese

1 cup blanched green peas

⅓ cup chopped Italian
(flat-leaf) parsley or chives

SALMON

4 pieces (each 6 oz) sockeye
salmon, skin on, deboned

3 Tbsp olive oil

Fleur de sel, for garnish

A RED WINE SAUCE can work well with salmon, and this one includes Pinot Noir and chicken stock as the main ingredients. The richness of the risotto is a wonderful balance for the smooth texture of the salmon. *Serves 4*

SAUCE: Combine wine, thyme, peppercorns, shallot and bay leaves in a saucepan on medium-high heat. Bring to a boil and cook for about 10 minutes, or until reduced by half. Add stock and cook for about 10 minutes, or until reduced by one-third. Strain through a fine-mesh sieve, then whisk in honey and butter. Season with salt. Keep warm.

RISOTTO: Place stock in a large pot on medium heat and bring to a gentle simmer. Keep hot.

In another pot, heat 4 Tbsp of the olive oil on medium heat. Sauté shallots until translucent (do not brown). Add rice and cook for 3 to 4 minutes, stirring until grains are coated with oil. Add wine, stir gently and cook until liquid is absorbed.

Add ½ cup of hot stock at a time, bring to a simmer and stir gently; wait until each addition is nearly all absorbed before adding more. Do not stir too often or too hard, as you risk breaking the grains. Continue this process until the risotto has cooked for about 15 minutes. At this point, the risotto should be al dente (firm and tender), moist and almost creamy.

To finish risotto, gently stir in Parmesan, butter and mascarpone. Fold in green peas and parsley (or chives). Season to taste with salt and freshly ground white pepper.

SALMON: Preheat the oven to 375°F. Season salmon with salt and freshly ground white pepper. Heat oil in an ovenproof frying pan on medium-high heat until oil ripples. Gently place salmon in frying pan, skin side down, and sear for 2 to 3 minutes, or until lightly browned. Carefully turn fish over, then place the pan in the oven and roast for 7 to 9 minutes, or until fish is done (flesh is opaque and flakes easily with a fork).

TO SERVE: Divide risotto among four warmed plates. Drizzle the 2 Tbsp of remaining olive oil over the risotto, then top each serving with a piece of salmon. Drizzle the sauce around the edge of the plate.

PAN-SEARED TROUT

WITH CAULIFLOWER PURÉE
AND POACHED OYSTERS

PURÉE

1 small cauliflower, in florets

2 bay leaves

2 Tbsp butter

4 cups (or more) milk

TROUT

2 Tbsp olive oil

4 pieces trout (each 7 oz), scaled and bones removed

OYSTERS

1½ cups white chicken stock (page 132)

10 beach oysters, shucked and cleaned

1 cup whipping cream

THIS DISH brings together childhood memories of trout fishing in the interior of British Columbia and my love of cooking. My dad used to cook trout that we caught with oysters that we'd brought with us. Instead of searing the oysters like my dad, I poach them. But, if you prefer, you can just pan-fry them to keep it simple. Try to remove as many bones as possible from the trout before you cook it. *Serves 4*

PURÉE: Place cauliflower, bay leaves and butter in a large saucepan and cover with milk (add more milk if needed). Bring to a boil on medium-high heat, then decrease the heat to medium and simmer for about 8 minutes, or until cauliflower is tender. Strain through a fine-mesh sieve. Set milk aside. Place cauliflower in a food processor with a little of the milk and process until smooth. Strain through a fine-mesh sieve.

TROUT: Heat oil in a frying pan on high heat. Season trout with salt and freshly ground white pepper. Place trout in the pan, skin side down, and cook for 3 to 4 minutes. Turn fish over and cook for 3 to 4 minutes, or until done (flesh is opaque and flakes easily with a fork). Remove trout from the pan.

OYSTERS: Place stock in a saucepan on medium-high heat and bring to a boil. Add 6 of the oysters and cook for about 2 minutes. Remove from heat and allow to cool for 15 minutes. Transfer to a food processor, add cream and blend until smooth. Keep warm.

Just before serving, strain through a fine-mesh sieve into a clean saucepan on medium heat. Cut the remaining oysters in half and add to the puréed oyster mixture. Cook for about 2 minutes to poach oysters lightly.

TO SERVE: Reheat the cauliflower purée, then season with salt and freshly ground white pepper. Divide the purée among four warmed plates and top with a piece of trout. Spoon the oyster mixture around the trout, making sure that each serving gets two pieces of oyster.

SEARED SKATE WINGS

WITH BROWN BUTTER SAUCE

AND GREEN BEANS

IN EUROPE, skate is served everywhere, but you don't see it on menus in North America very often. That's too bad, because skate is very versatile, tasty and not expensive. Make sure the skate is cooked through, or the flesh will not come off the bone. And when you're making the brown butter sauce, watch out, as the hot butter could splatter you when you add the lemon juice. *Serves 4*

SKATE AND GREEN BEANS: Fill a bowl with ice water. Bring a saucepan of salted water to a boil. Blanch green beans by placing in the boiling water for 20 to 30 seconds. Take out green beans and immediately put them into the ice water to stop the cooking. When green beans are cool, take them out of the ice water and drain on paper towels.

Preheat the oven to 375°F. Lightly cover a baking sheet with flour. Dredge skate wings in flour on both sides and place on a clean plate. Season with salt and freshly cracked white pepper.

Melt butter in a large frying pan on medium-high heat. When the pan is lightly smoking, add skate wings and cook for 2 minutes on each side, or until golden brown. Transfer skate to a clean baking sheet. Place in the oven and bake for 2 to 3 minutes, or until done (when the flesh is coming off the bone). Remove from the oven.

Heat the oil in another large frying pan on medium heat. Add bacon and shallots, then cook for 1 to 2 minutes, or until softened. Add green beans, then season with salt and freshly ground white pepper. Cook for 1 to 1½ minutes, or until green beans are warmed through. Remove from the stove.

SAUCE: Melt butter in a small saucepan on medium-high heat until it starts to foam. Remove from the stove, then stir in lemon juice, parsley and capers. Season with salt and freshly ground white pepper.

TO SERVE: Divide green beans among four warmed plates and place a skate wing on top of each. Spoon a generous amount of brown butter sauce onto each skate wing. Lightly drizzle aged balsamic vinegar (optional) over each serving.

SKATE AND GREEN BEANS

1 lb green beans, trimmed

⅓ cup all-purpose flour

4 skate wings

2 Tbsp butter

1 Tbsp extra-virgin olive oil

3 or 4 slices good-quality bacon, thinly sliced

6 shallots, thinly sliced

SAUCE

6 Tbsp unsalted butter

2 Tbsp fresh lemon juice

2 Tbsp chopped parsley

1 Tbsp drained capers

Aged balsamic vinegar (optional)

CRAB RAVIOLI

THIS IS ONE of the dishes we prepared on *Iron Chef America*—it was a hit with all the judges. We use Japanese mayonnaise because it is made with rice vinegar, so it is more tart than traditional mayonnaise. Together with the Japanese herb shiso (page 37), they make a perfect foil for the crab. These two ingredients make all the difference in the final dish. *Serves 4*

FILLING: Mix together all the filling ingredients in a bowl. The amount of Japanese mayonnaise depends on the moisture content of the crabmeat—use just enough to bind the mixture. The amount of shiso depends on the size of the leaves.

Stuff the ravioli according to the instructions with the pasta dough recipe.

BEURRE BLANC: Combine rice vinegar and wine in a saucepan on medium heat, then reduce until the liquid forms a light syrup. (If you are not experienced at making butter sauces, you can prevent the sauce from splitting by adding the optional cream.) Decrease the heat to low and whisk in butter, one piece at a time, until well incorporated. Add lemon juice, truffle oil and truffle (or an additional ¼ tsp truffle oil). Season to taste with salt. Set aside and keep warm. When reheating, be careful not to boil the sauce as it may split.

TO SERVE: Divide ravioli among four warmed plates and top each serving with ¼ cup of the black truffle beurre blanc. Drizzle each plate with extra-virgin olive oil and top each ravioli with a grain of fleur de sel. Sprinkle with chervil.

Pasta dough with semolina (page 138)

FILLING

1 lb crabmeat

2 Tbsp minced ginger

2 Tbsp minced shallots

⅓ to ½ cup Japanese mayonnaise

2 to 3 shiso leaves, minced

2 cloves garlic, minced

BEURRE BLANC

⅓ cup rice vinegar

⅛ cup dry white wine

1 tsp whipping cream (optional)

⅓ cup unsalted butter, ½-inch cubes, chilled

1 Tbsp fresh lemon juice

¼ tsp white truffle oil

1 Tbsp finely chopped black truffle or ¼ tsp white truffle oil

GARNISH

Extra-virgin olive oil

Fleur de sel

Chopped chervil

GRILLED LOBSTER

WITH GARLIC BUTTER
AND SAUCE VERTE

SAUCE VERTE

1½ tsp grapeseed oil

1 Tbsp white wine vinegar

3 Tbsp Dijon mustard

¼ cup drained capers,
rinsed and roughly chopped

3 Tbsp finely chopped
fresh tarragon

3 Tbsp finely chopped
fresh basil

2 Tbsp finely chopped fresh
Italian (flat-leaf) parsley

¼ cup finely chopped spinach

1 clove garlic, minced

1 Tbsp fresh lemon juice

LOBSTER

4 live lobsters (each 1½ lbs)

Lemon slices, for garnish

GARLIC BUTTER

½ lb unsalted butter

2 cloves garlic,
coarsely chopped

1 Tbsp fresh lemon juice

WHEN YOU BUY LOBSTER, the best size is 1 to 1½ lbs. It is important not to cook the lobster in boiling water for more than 2 minutes and to immerse it immediately in ice water to stop the cooking. Nobody likes a chewy lobster. Nothing goes better with lobster than garlic and butter. *Serves 4*

SAUCE VERTE: Whisk together oil, vinegar and mustard in a small bowl. Stir in the remaining ingredients. Cover and refrigerate until needed.

LOBSTER: Fill a large bowl with ice water. Bring a large stockpot filled with water to a boil on high heat. Put in lobsters and cook for 2 minutes. Take out lobsters and immediately plunge them into the ice water. When lobsters are completely cool, take them out of the water. Use a large, heavy knife to split each lobster in half lengthwise. Refrigerate lobsters until needed.

GARLIC BUTTER: Place butter, garlic and lemon juice in a small saucepan on low heat. When butter melts, stir the mixture well. Keep warm.

FINISH LOBSTERS: Oil the grill lightly, then preheat the barbecue on medium to high heat (between 400°F and 425°F). Spoon garlic butter over the cut side of lobsters. Grill lobsters, cut side up, for 8 to 10 minutes, or until done (meat is opaque and is slightly firm to the touch).

TO SERVE: Place two lobster halves on each warmed plate and drizzle with sauce verte. Garnish with slices of lemon on the side.

CLAM AND
PANCETTA SAUCE
WITH LINGUINE

12 oz dry spaghetti or linguine

4 Tbsp extra-virgin olive oil

1 cup diced (¼ inch) pancetta

1 tsp minced garlic

1 lb Manila clams, cleaned

1 cup dry white wine

2 Tbsp unsalted butter

¼ cup finely chopped
Italian (flat-leaf) parsley

WHAT I LOVE about this dish is all the beautiful clam nectar that gets tossed with the pasta. Be sure to purchase fresh clams the same day you make this dish, to discard any unopened clams once they are cooked and that the pasta is al dente when you add it to the sauce. Both the pancetta and the clams are naturally salty, so it is unlikely you will need any additional salt. *Serves 4*

Bring a stockpot of salted water to a boil. Add spaghettini and cook for 5 to 6 minutes, or until almost al dente. Drain in a colander.

Heat 2 Tbsp of the oil in a large saucepan on medium heat. Add pancetta and garlic, then sauté for about 8 minutes, or until golden brown. Add clams, wine and butter. Cover the pan with a tight-fitting lid and cook for about 10 minutes, or until the clams open. Remove from the stove. Take out clams, remove the meat and discard the shells. Strain the cooking liquid through a fine-mesh sieve into a clean saucepan and set aside the pancetta. Keep clam meat and pancetta warm.

Place the saucepan with the cooking liquid on high heat and cook for about 5 minutes, or until reduced by half. Add clam meat, pancetta and pasta, then cook for 2 to 3 minutes. Add parsley and the remaining oil, then toss gently.

TO SERVE: Transfer pasta and sauce to a large bowl so that guests can help themselves.

BRAISED LAMB SHANK

THIS IS probably one of my favourite dishes in the entire book and, conveniently, it is also one of the simplest to prepare. Just like those gorgeous Italian dishes with pasta and braised meat, this combination of rich lamb, dark jus and sharp Parmesan is pure heaven. *Serves 4*

Heat 2 Tbsp of the oil in a medium stockpot on high heat, until smoking. Season lamb with salt and freshly ground white pepper, then sear on all sides for about 10 minutes, or until golden brown. Take lamb out of the stockpot.

Add the remaining oil to the stockpot. Add shallots and cook on medium heat for about 10 minutes, or until lightly caramelized. Add lamb, garlic, wine, water, bay leaves, pepper-corns, thyme and parsley. Increase the heat to high and bring to a boil, then decrease the heat to medium and simmer for 1½ to 2 hours, or until meat falls off the bone. Transfer lamb to a platter and cover with aluminium foil to keep warm.

Cook the liquid in the stockpot on high heat for about 30 minutes, or until reduced by half, skimming off oil from the surface every 15 minutes. Strain the reduced liquid through a fine-mesh sieve and discard the solids.

Take lamb meat off the bone and discard bones. Use your hands to coarsely shred meat. Place meat and the strained liquid in a large frying pan on medium heat and bring to a simmer.

Bring a large pot of salted water to a boil on high heat. Add rigatoni and cook for about 6 minutes, or until al dente. Drain and add to the lamb. Toss well and add parsley.

TO SERVE: Divide lamb and pasta into four warmed bowls. Place Parmesan in a bowl on the side for guests to help themselves.

4 Tbsp extra-virgin olive oil

6 lamb shanks

5 to 6 shallots, thinly sliced

1 head garlic,
cut in half horizontally

1 cup dry red wine

2 quarts cold water

2 bay leaves

10 black peppercorns

6 sprigs fresh thyme

6 sprigs fresh parsley

1 lb dried rigatoni

¼ cup coarsely chopped
Italian (flat-leaf) parsley

½ cup grated Parmesan

ONE OF THE THINGS I love about the cuisine of southern France is its use of garlic, olives, tomatoes and broth. This dish is packed with flavour, but it is still very light. This sauce also goes perfectly with halibut, sablefish or even lobster. Traditionally, in this region, the sauces are finished with a drizzle of extra-virgin oil, but if you want a richer taste, use butter instead. *Serves 4*

Preheat the oven to 400°F. Rub red bell pepper with a little vegetable oil, place in a baking pan and roast in the oven for 15 to 20 minutes, until skin is blistered. Leave the oven on, but remove red pepper and transfer to a bowl, cover with plastic wrap and let sit for 10 minutes so skin will loosen. Peel red pepper, remove and discard seeds, then chop coarsely.

Season chicken generously with salt and freshly ground white pepper. Heat olive oil in a large ovenproof frying pan on high heat. Add chicken legs, skin side down, and sear for 2 to 3 minutes, or until golden. Turn chicken over. Place the pan in the oven for about 25 minutes, basting every 5 minutes with drippings, until done (juice should be clear when pricked with the point of a sharp knife). Remove from the oven and allow to rest so that juice stays in the meat.

To make the sauce, place stock, roasted red pepper, capers, olives and garlic in a large saucepan on high heat. (Do not use a small pan, as you will be reducing the sauce, and a larger surface area will speed up this process.) Cook for about 3 minutes, or until stock is reduced by half. Just before serving, gently stir in mixed herbs, oil and tomatoes. Season with salt and freshly ground white pepper.

TO SERVE: Place a piece of chicken in each of four warmed bowls. Spoon sauce over chicken, making sure that each serving gets 2 tomato halves. If you wish, drizzle a little extra-virgin olive oil (optional) over each serving.

1 red bell pepper

4 large chicken legs, thighs attached

1 tsp olive oil

2 cups dark chicken stock (page 132)

2 Tbsp drained capers

¼ cup pitted and halved kalamata olives

1 tsp minced garlic

⅓ cup mixed herbs (equal amounts of parsley, chives, tarragon)

1 Tbsp extra-virgin olive oil

4 butter-braised tomatoes (page 31), cut in half

Extra-virgin olive oil, for garnish (optional)

HONEY-GLAZED DUCK

WITH ORANGE GNOCCHI, LEEK-FENNEL
FONDANT AND ORANGE ROSEMARY JUS

Orange gnocchi
(page 105)

JUS
¾ cup sugar

1 cup water

¾ cup orange juice

3 Tbsp apple cider vinegar

4 shallots, chopped

2 cloves garlic, chopped

1 orange, zest only

2 sprigs fresh thyme

2 sprigs fresh rosemary

2 quarts duck stock (page 132)

FONDANT
1 large bulb fennel,
halved and cored

2 leeks, white parts only

2 Tbsp canola oil

½ cup dry white wine

½ cup white chicken
stock (page 132)

2 Tbsp unsalted butter

DUCK
6 duck breast halves

2 Tbsp canola oil

3 Tbsp honey

1 Tbsp fresh thyme leaves

THIS IS OUR TAKE on the classic duck à l'orange. If you're using a Peking duck, pull out the fat under the skin to ensure that it will be gorgeously crispy. The other thing I love about this dish is the fondant—and also that the gnocchi can be made ahead. *Serves 6*

JUS: Place sugar and water in a medium-sized, heavy-bottomed saucepan on medium-high heat and cook (do not stir or sugar will crystallize) for about 10 minutes, or until dark amber. Immediately stir in orange juice and vinegar, then cook for about 10 minutes, or until the liquid is reduced by half.

Add shallots, garlic, orange zest, thyme, rosemary and stock, then bring to a boil on high heat and cook for about 30 minutes, or until reduced by half. Strain through a fine-mesh sieve into a bowl and discard the solids. Keep the jus warm.

FONDANT: Cut fennel into very thin slices (use a mandoline if you have one).

Slice leeks once lengthwise, then cut into half rounds ¼-inch thick. Wash well to remove any grit.

Heat oil in a frying pan on medium heat. Add fennel and cook for about 10 minutes, until starting to soften. Add leek and cook for about 5 minutes, or until starting to soften. Season with salt and freshly ground white pepper. Add wine and stir to deglaze the bottom of the pan. Add stock and cook for about 10 minutes, or until most of the liquid is gone. Add butter and stir until melted. Remove from the stove and set aside in a warm place.

DUCK: Preheat the oven to 450°F. Use a knife to score the fatty side of each duck breast, to a depth of ¼ inch, but be careful not to puncture the flesh. Season with salt and freshly ground white pepper.

Heat oil in a large ovenproof frying pan on medium heat. Arrange duck breasts in the pan, fat side down, and cook for about 5 minutes, or until fat is golden brown. Place the pan in the oven for 5 to 7 minutes, or until breasts are medium-rare (a little pink juice comes out when you press on the duck). Be careful when you take the duck out of the oven, as the fat may spit.

Heat honey and thyme in a small saucepan on high heat for about 5 minutes, or until thyme is fragrant and honey is starting to darken. Dip the fat side of each duck breast in the honey mixture, then place on a paper towel, fat side up, to rest.

TO SERVE: Cook the gnocchi (page 105). Divide fondant among six warmed plates. Arrange gnocchi beside the fondant. Slice duck breasts and arrange on top of the fondant. Spoon some jus around the fondant.

MAPLE-GLAZED PORK BELLY

WITH NAVY BEAN PURÉE

AND APPLE-BACON COMPOTE

THIS IS one of the most decadent braised dishes that you can make—and you can cook the pork, and even the whole thing, a day ahead. Pork belly is unsmoked, uncured side bacon in one piece. Ask your butcher to cut a piece the size you need. We add a soft bean purée for a tasty twist on the traditional pork and beans, and to cut the richness of the pork, we add sherry vinegar and apple. *Serves 6*

PORK BELLY: Preheat the oven to 325°F. Heat oil in a large frying pan on medium to medium-high heat. Add carrots, celery, onions, lemon grass, ginger and garlic, then sauté for about 10 minutes, or until softened. Transfer to a hot roasting pan and add pork belly, fat side up. Add stock, soy sauce, thyme, peppercorns and bay leaves. Cover with a lid or aluminum foil, then cook in the oven for 4½ hours. Remove from the oven and allow pork to cool in the cooking liquid.

When pork is cool, take it out of the cooking liquid. Save the liquid and refrigerate until needed.

Place a cooling rack in a shallow pan and cover the rack with parchment paper. Put pork on top of the parchment paper. Put another piece of parchment paper on top of the pork, then cover with another shallow pan. Put 4 to 5 tins of canned food inside the shallow pan that's on top of the pork, in order to press it, and refrigerate overnight.

COMPOTE: Heat oil in a frying pan on medium heat. Add bacon and apples, then sauté for 5 to 7 minutes, or until apples soften. Add honey and maple syrup, then cook for 8 to 10 minutes, or until apples are caramelized. Add vinegar and stir to deglaze the bottom of the pan. Cook for 4 to 5 minutes, or until liquid is reduced to syrup. Season with salt and freshly ground white pepper. Can be made a day ahead.

recipe continued overleaf >

PORK BELLY

4 Tbsp canola oil

1 cup ½-inch dice carrots

1 cup ½-inch dice celery

1 cup ½-inch dice onions

¼ cup ¼-inch dice lemon grass

¼ cup minced ginger

2 cloves garlic

3 lbs pork belly

4 quarts white chicken stock (page 132)

1 cup light soy sauce

8 sprigs fresh thyme

1 tsp black peppercorns

3 bay leaves

½ cup maple syrup

Chervil, for garnish

COMPOTE

4 Tbsp olive oil

8 oz Irish bacon, ¼-inch dice

4 Gala apples, peeled, cored and ½-inch dice

2 Tbsp liquid honey

3 Tbsp maple syrup

1 cup sherry vinegar

PURÉE

2 cups navy beans, soaked overnight in 6 cups cold water

3 quarts white chicken stock (page 132)

2 stalks celery

1 onion

2 bay leaves

3½ oz bacon

4 Tbsp butter

¼ to ½ cup whipping cream

PURÉE: Drain and rinse beans. Place beans, stock, celery, onion, bay leaves and bacon in a saucepan on medium-low heat and simmer for about 90 minutes, or until beans are tender. Remove and discard celery, onion, bay leaves and bacon. Save the cooking liquid.

Place beans in a food processor and purée, adding ⅓ to ⅔ cup of the reserved bean-cooking liquid, just enough to ease the puréeing. Strain bean purée through a fine-mesh sieve. Season with salt and freshly ground white pepper. Can be made a day ahead up to this point.

FINISH PORK: Preheat the oven to 350°F. Cut the pressed pork into 6 portions. Pour maple syrup and enough of the reserved pork-cooking liquid into an ovenproof frying pan to cover the bottom to a depth of ½ inch. Place the pan on the stove on medium heat until liquid is warmed through, then place in the oven and heat pork belly for 7 to 10 minutes, basting often with the cooking liquid until warmed through. Remove from the oven.

TO SERVE: Add butter and cream to bean purée and reheat. Reheat apple-bacon compote. Place ¾ cup of the bean purée in the middle of each of six warmed plates and top with a piece of pork belly. Drizzle with some of the cooking liquid from the frying pan. Place 3 Tbsp warm compote on top of each piece of pork. Garnish with chervil.

VEAL NEPTUNE

WITH CRAB HOLLANDAISE
AND MUSHROOM RAGOUT

RAGOUT

4 Tbsp canola oil

12 pearl onions, peeled

3 Tbsp sherry vinegar

6 Tbsp butter

2 lbs shimeji mushrooms, trimmed

1 cup Peking duck broth (page 135)

VEAL

2 lbs veal loin

4 Tbsp canola oil

CRAB HOLLANDAISE

2 egg yolks

½ lemon, juice of

¼ cup Riesling

1 cup clarified butter (page 136)

4 oz crabmeat

Extra-virgin olive oil, for garnish

Sea salt, for garnish

Chervil, for garnish

THIS WAS one of the dishes that helped us win on *Iron Chef America*. We managed to pull it off in just 1 hour, but it is better if you can take more time to make the hollandaise and the mushroom ragout. You can make the Peking duck broth in advance. *Serves 4*

RAGOUT: Heat 2 Tbsp of the oil in a frying pan on medium-high heat. Add pearl onions and sauté, stirring occasionally, for 7 to 10 minutes, or until golden brown. Add vinegar and stir to deglaze the bottom of the pan. Cook for 4 to 5 minutes, or until liquid is reduced to a syrup. Remove from the stove.

Heat the rest of the oil and 2 Tbsp of the butter in another frying pan on medium-high heat until butter is foamy. Add mushrooms and sauté for 5 to 7 minutes, or until golden brown and wilted. Add pearl onions and their cooking liquid, then cook for 1 minute. Add broth and stir to deglaze the bottom of the pan. Cook for 5 to 7 minutes, or until reduced by three-quarters. Stir in the remaining butter and keep warm.

VEAL: Preheat the oven to 425°F. Trim veal loin of excessive fat and silver skin (the tough pearl-coloured membrane). Season with salt and freshly ground white pepper. Heat oil in an ovenproof frying pan on medium-high heat. Sear veal for 2 to 3 minutes on each side, or until well browned. Discard any excess oil from the pan. Place the pan in the oven and roast the veal for 10 to 15 minutes, or until medium-rare (130°F/55°C on a meat thermometer). Remove from the oven and allow to rest for 7 to 10 minutes. (While the veal is resting, make the crab hollandaise.) Carve veal into slices ¼-inch thick.

CRAB HOLLANDAISE: Place egg yolks, lemon juice and wine in a bain marie (a bowl set in a pan of very hot water) and whisk constantly for 5 to 7 minutes, or until thick. Place clarified butter in a saucepan on medium-low heat and warm it up. Slowly add clarified butter to the egg mixture, whisking all the while. Remove the hollandaise sauce from the heat, then season with salt and freshly ground white pepper. Fold in crabmeat.

TO SERVE: Place the mushroom ragout with some of its reduced sauce in the centre of each of four warmed plates. Place equal amounts of veal on top of mushrooms for each serving. Top with the crabmeat hollandaise. Garnish with olive oil, sea salt and chervil.

STEAK AND
BLUE CHEESE PIE

BOUQUET GARNI

1 carrot, diced

2 stalks celery, diced

1 onion, diced

4 cloves garlic

2 sprigs fresh thyme

1 sprig fresh rosemary

1 sprig fresh sage

5 black peppercorns

1 bay leaf

STEAK PIE

1 sheet frozen
puff pastry, thawed

2 lbs top sirloin, 1-inch cubes

1 bottle (26 oz) dry red wine

1 cup or more canola oil

3 cups veal stock (page 134)

7 oz double-smoked bacon,
1-inch wide strips

1 lb mushrooms, quartered

2 cups peeled pearl onions

¾ cup butter

¾ cup flour

14 oz blue cheese
(your favourite kind)

I HAVE ALWAYS LIKED traditional steak and kidney pie, so I wanted to create something similar, but with a twist. The diners at Feenie's love this dish. It's actually more like a *bourguignon,* but with blue cheese, and it has less "crust" than a steak and kidney pie. *Serves 4 to 6*

BOUQUET GARNI: Place all ingredients on a 6-inch square of cheesecloth and tie closed with kitchen string.

STEAK PIE: Roll out puff pastry to a thickness of ⅛ inch, then use a 5-inch diameter cutter to cut out 4 to 6 rounds. Cover and refrigerate.

Place bouquet garni, meat and wine in a deep container. Cover and marinate overnight in the refrigerator.

Preheat the oven to 325°F. Take out meat and the bouquet garni from wine. Pat meat dry with paper towels, then season with salt and freshly ground white pepper. Set aside the bouquet garni and wine separately.

Heat ¼ cup of the oil in a frying pan on medium-high heat. Add meat in small batches and brown, using more oil if necessary, then place in a deep casserole dish.

Meanwhile, place the stock and reserved wine in a saucepan on high heat and bring to a simmer. Skim off and discard any impurities, then add wine mixture and reserved bouquet garni to browned meat. Cover the casserole dish with aluminum foil. Place in the oven and cook for 1½ to 2 hours, or until meat is tender.

While meat is cooking, sauté bacon in a frying pan on medium heat for about 8 minutes, or until crispy. Drain bacon on paper towels. Keep the pan and bacon fat on the stove and decrease the heat to low. Add mushrooms and sauté for about 5 minutes, or until browned and no liquid remains in the pan. Season with salt and freshly ground white pepper.

In another frying pan, heat 3 Tbsp of the oil on medium heat. Add pearl onions and sauté for about 10 minutes, or until cooked through and lightly caramelized. Season with salt and freshly ground white pepper.

When meat is cooked, take it out of the cooking liquid and set aside. Keep braising liquid and discard sachet.

In a clean saucepan, melt butter on medium heat. Add flour all at once and cook, stirring constantly, for about 5 minutes, or until mixture thickens and is fairly dry. With the pan on medium to medium-low heat, slowly add the cooking liquid, stirring constantly. When all the liquid has been added, cook, stirring well, for about 10 minutes, or until it thickens, then increase the heat to high and bring to a boil for 2 minutes. Remove from the stove and strain through a fine-mesh sieve into a clean saucepan. Season with salt and freshly ground white pepper. Add reserved meat, onions, mushrooms and bacon. Keep hot.

FINISH PIE: Preheat the oven to 450°F. Line a baking sheet with parchment paper. Place half of the blue cheese in a dish and microwave on medium heat, 30 seconds at a time, stirring after each time, until completely melted. Brush melted cheese on the tops of the pastry rounds and place them on the prepared baking sheet. Refrigerate for 10 minutes, then bake in the oven for 6 to 10 minutes, or until pastry is puffed and browned.

TO SERVE: Divide meat mixture into bowls and garnish with chunks of the remaining blue cheese. Place a round of puff pastry on top of each serving.

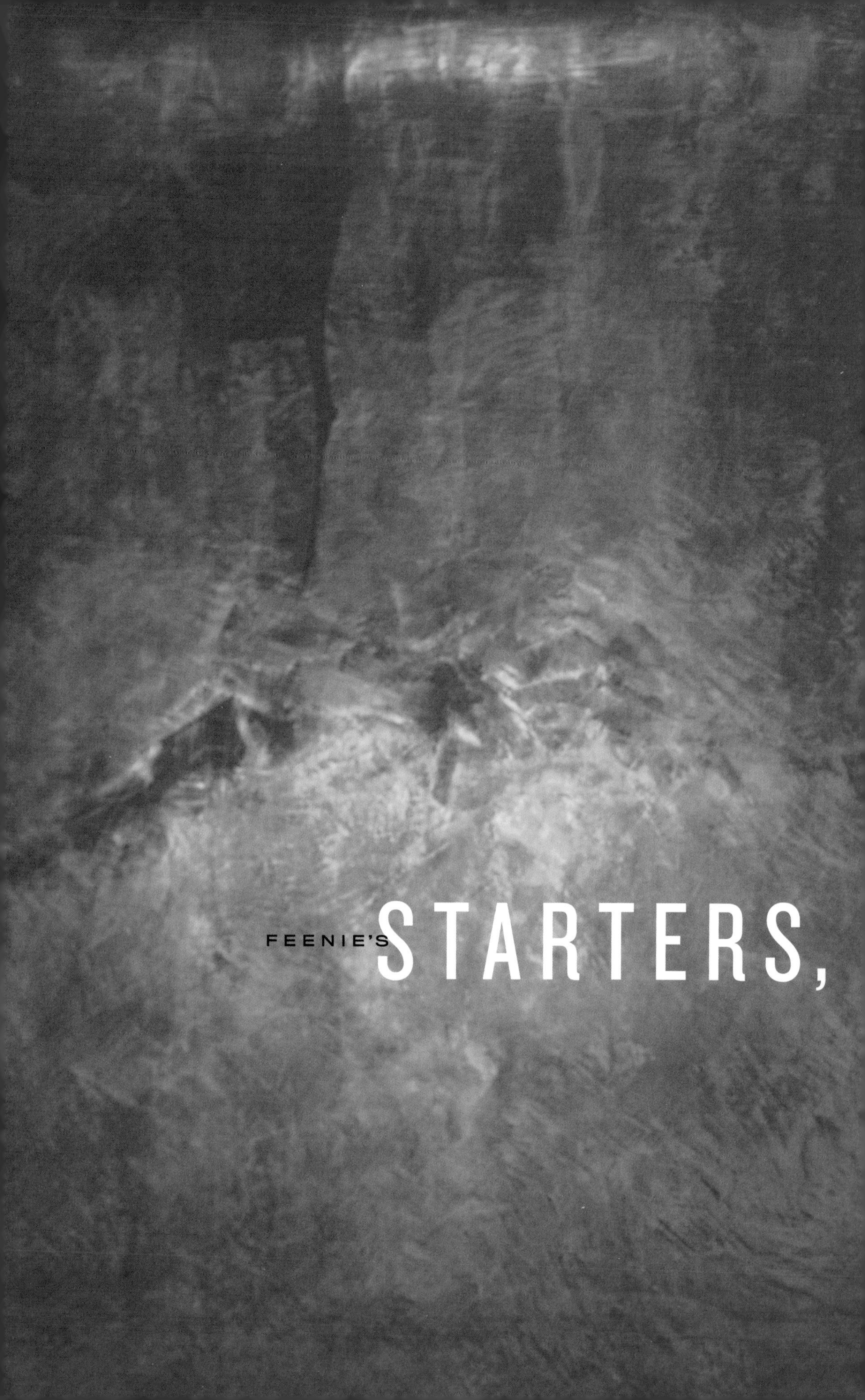

FEENIE'S STARTERS,

SOUPS & SALADS

CRAB, SMOKED TUNA AND
SMOKED SALMON SUSHI ROLLS

SUSHI

1 ripe mango

1 cucumber

1 shiso leaf (page 37)

¾ lb Dungeness crabmeat

½ cup Japanese
mayonnaise (page 49)

2 Tbsp yuzu juice (page 100)

1 lb smoked salmon, sliced

2 sheets of nori

1 lb smoked albacore
tuna, sliced

VINAIGRETTE

2 Tbsp grainy mustard

½ Tbsp soy sauce

2 Tbsp Japanese rice vinegar

6 Tbsp extra-virgin olive oil

GARNISH

4 Tbsp crème fraîche
(page 136)

Salmon roe

Baby watercress

ONE OF MY first thoughts when we competed in *Iron Chef America* was that I wanted to give the judges our version of British Columbia/Japanese cuisine. Here, Dungeness crab with tropical mango and our wonderful local smoked salmon represents the fantastic blend of West Coast products and Japanese technique that Vancouver is becoming so well known for. The most important thing to remember when making this dish is to prepare and serve it the same day. *Serves 6*

SUSHI: Peel and cut mango into batons (or sticks) ¼-inch thick and as long as possible.

Peel cucumber, cut in half lengthwise and deseed. Cut into batons ¼-inch thick. Thinly slice shiso leaf.

Place crab, cucumber and shiso in a bowl and mix together. Add Japanese mayonnaise and yuzu juice a little at a time, until the mixture makes a moist salad. Season with salt and freshly ground white pepper.

Line a sushi-rolling mat with plastic wrap, with the long edge at the bottom. On it, place smoked salmon slices to cover the plastic, leaving about 1½ inches free along the left and right. Cut a sheet of nori to cover the salmon and place on top. Cover the nori sheet with half of the crabmeat. Place a row of mango batons lengthwise along the bottom edge of the nori. From the bottom, carefully roll up into a cylinder, then tuck in the salmon ends. Tighten the plastic wrap, twist the ends closed and refrigerate.

Follow the same procedure using the smoked tuna in place of the salmon.

VINAIGRETTE: Place all the ingredients in a bowl and whisk together.

TO SERVE: Cut each roll into slices of desired thickness. Place one slice of each roll on six chilled plates. Drizzle mustard vinaigrette around each plate. Garnish with crème fraîche, salmon roe and watercress leaves.

SCALLOP
CARPACCIO

4 large scallops

6 Tbsp extra-virgin olive oil

2 Tbsp cilantro oil (page 137)

Pinch of fleur de sel

1 tsp finely chopped
jalapeño pepper

¼ cup tomato concassé
(page 137)

1 Tbsp finely sliced
fresh mint leaves

1 Tbsp finely sliced cilantro

1 lime, juice only

1 lemon, juice only

FOR THIS DISH, buy the freshest scallops you can find. Here, I match scallops with both lime and lemon, as well as with cilantro oil and interesting herbs and spices. *Serves 4*

Cut each scallop horizontally into 4 thin slices and arrange on four chilled plates. Cover with plastic wrap and refrigerate until needed.

TO SERVE: Remove the plastic wrap from the plates. Drizzle 1½ Tbsp extra-virgin olive oil over each serving of scallops, making sure each slice is coated. Drizzle cilantro oil over scallops.

Season with fleur de sel and freshly ground white pepper. Sprinkle jalapeño, tomato, mint and cilantro over each scallop slice. Sprinkle with lemon juice and lime juice.

SEARED PRAWNS
IN PERNOD

IS THERE ANYTHING TASTIER than shellfish and alcohol? The strong anise flavour of the Pernod combined with the sweetness of the fresh prawns takes me back to France. You can never make too much of this dish for a dinner party. Just serve it with a crusty baguette and you're all set! *Serves 4*

Heat oil in a frying pan on high heat. Season prawns with salt and freshly ground white pepper. Add prawns and sear on one side for about 2 minutes. Turn prawns, add garlic, and sear prawns for about 2 minutes, or until they turn bright pink. Transfer prawns to a warmed serving plate, but leave the pan on the stove.

Add Pernod (or Ricard) and stir to deglaze the bottom of the pan. Allow to boil for 1 minute, then remove from the stove. Whisk in butter, tarragon, parsley, chives and chervil.

TO SERVE: Pour any juice released by prawns into the Pernod sauce and stir in. Spoon Pernod sauce over prawns.

3 Tbsp olive oil

12 prawns, peeled and deveined

1 tsp minced garlic

2 Tbsp Pernod or Ricard

1 Tbsp unsalted butter

1 Tbsp chopped fresh tarragon

1 Tbsp chopped fresh parsley

1 Tbsp chopped fresh chives

1 Tbsp chopped fresh chervil

SEARED SCALLOPS

BECAUSE scallops have a beautiful sweet flavour, we've combined them, for contrast, with radicchio, which is slightly bitter. Be careful not to go overboard with the lemon juice, as you also have the juice from the pink grapefruit segments. *Serves 4*

Preheat the oven to 400°F.

Melt butter in a frying pan on medium heat. Add radicchio and cook for about 3 minutes, or until wilted. Add grapefruit and warm for 30 seconds on each side. Add lemon juice and parsley. Remove from the stove.

Season scallops with salt and freshly ground white pepper. Heat oil in an ovenproof frying pan on high heat. Add scallops and sear on one side for about 2 minutes, or until dark golden brown. Turn scallops over, place the pan in the oven and cook for 2 minutes, or until done. We like them medium-rare (the scallop still gives a little when squeezed between a finger and thumb).

TO SERVE: Divide radicchio-grapefruit mixture among four warmed plates. Top each serving with a scallop.

1 Tbsp unsalted butter

¼ cup shredded radicchio

1 pink grapefruit, peeled segments only

1 lemon, juice only

2 Tbsp chopped Italian (flat-leaf) parsley

4 large scallops

1 Tbsp olive oil

PEKING DUCK TERRINE

PANCAKE

1⅔ cups flour

3 green onions, finely chopped

½ cup + 2 tsp boiling water

1 tsp sesame oil

TERRINE

1 tsp canola oil

2 cups duck stock (page 132), including cooking juice from duck cavities

2 whole Chinese barbecued ducks (not cut up)

1 quart rendered duck fat (page 135)

4 whole star anise

½ stick of cinnamon

8 Szechwan peppercorns

6 cloves garlic

1 bunch green onions

3 Tbsp hoisin sauce

1 can (8 oz) sliced water chestnuts, drained

TERRINES are very time-consuming, but this one is worth the effort if you are lucky enough to live in a place with a Chinatown so that you can buy the Chinese barbecued duck. At Feenie's, we serve this terrine with pea shoots and some diced Asian pear dressed with sesame oil. Be sure to save the duck carcasses (wrap them in plastic and freeze until needed) to make Peking duck broth (page 135). *Serves 12 to 14*

PANCAKE: Toss together flour and green onions in a bowl, until onions are well coated. Pour boiling water over the mixture, stirring until a firm dough forms. Add sesame oil and knead dough, on a lightly floured surface, for 5 minutes, until smooth in texture. Wrap dough in plastic wrap and place in the refrigerator to rest for 30 minutes.

On a lightly floured surface, roll out the dough into a rectangle 18 × 13 inches and about ¹⁄₁₆-inch thick. Brush off any excess flour.

Place the pancake on a dry, flat-top griddle on medium heat, and cook for 2 minutes or less, or until small brown circles appear on the bottom. Turn pancake over carefully, then cook for about 2 minutes, or until slightly puffed and pocked with brown flecks. Remove the griddle from the stove and cover the pancake with parchment paper in order to steam it. Allow to cool.

TERRINE: Lightly oil a terrine mould 10 × 3 × 3 inches, then carefully line it with plastic wrap, pressing out any air bubbles. Make sure that there is excess wrap hanging over the edges of the terrine.

Collect cooking juice from the cavities of the ducks. Place cooking juice and stock in a saucepan on high heat, then cook for about 30 minutes, until only 4 Tbsp remain.

Carefully remove the skin from ducks (in one piece if possible). Start along the backbone and work your way forward, running your finger between the skin and the flesh. When skin is off, scrape away any fat from it. Set aside the skins.

Preheat the oven to 325°F. Cut off the legs, thighs and breast meat from ducks. Place legs, thighs and breast meat

in an ovenproof dish. Warm duck fat on medium heat and pour over duck pieces. Add star anise, cinnamon, peppercorns and garlic.

Place the ovenproof dish on medium-high heat and bring fat to a boil, then cover the dish with aluminum foil and cook in the oven for 1 hour, or until the meat falls off the bone. Remove duck meat from fat and allow to cool. Strain fat through a sieve and set aside 1 cup. (You can reuse the remainder for another duck terrine or duck confit; it will keep in the refrigerator for months.)

Trim off and discard root ends of green onions. Fill a bowl with ice water. Bring a saucepan of salted water to a boil. Blanch green onions by cooking them in the boiling water for 2 minutes. Take out green onions and immediately plunge them into the ice water. Drain and pat dry with paper towels.

recipe continued overleaf >

TO ASSEMBLE: Line the prepared terrine mould with the mandarin pancake, trimming off any excess from the corners so that the pancake does not bunch up. The edges of the pancake should hang over the edges the terrine. Brush hoisin sauce over the inside of the pancake. Line the inside of the pancake with the duck skins, fat side in.

Remove duck meat from bones, then place meat in a food processor with a paddle attachment and break up into chunks. Add the cup of reserved cold duck fat and the reduced duck stock. Mix gently.

Place a third of the duck mixture in the bottom of the terrine, pressing down well and making sure that it is flat. Arrange half of the green onions lengthwise, all running in the same direction, on top of the duck meat.

Add a second layer of green onions, with their white parts at the opposite end to the first layer of green onions. Cover with a third of the duck meat and press down well, making sure it is flat.

Add a layer of water chestnuts, overlapping the slices to completely cover the duck meat. Add the remaining duck meat and press down firmly, making sure it is flat.

Fold the duck skin over the meat, then fold the pancake over the duck skin. Fold the plastic wrap over the pancake so that it holds the terrine together firmly. Cut a piece of cardboard to just fit on top of the terrine, then place a 2-lb weight (two packages of butter work well) on top of the cardboard. Carefully wrap the entire terrine mould and the weights in many layers of plastic wrap, place in the refrigerator upside down and leave overnight.

TO SERVE: Remove the outer plastic wrap, weights and cardboard from the terrine. Remove the terrine from the mould, but leave it in its layer of plastic wrap. Cut into slices ½-inch thick and place on a chilled platter. Remove the plastic wrap from the slices before serving.

BEEF CARPACCIO

WITH HORSERADISH
AND MUSTARD CREAM

THE MOST IMPORTANT THING with this dish is to slice the beef as thinly as possible after refrigerating it. *Serves 4*

CREAM: Whisk together crème fraîche, horseradish and mustard in a bowl. Season with a little salt. Cover and refrigerate until needed.

MARINADE: Place rice and sherry vinegars, garlic, capers, shallot, mustard, parsley, rosemary and thyme in a food processor. Process while slowly adding oil until creamy. Transfer to a bowl.

CARPACCIO: Season beef with salt and freshly ground white pepper. Heat oil in a large frying pan on high heat. Add beef and sear on each side for 10 seconds. Remove from the stove and roll beef in the marinade. Allow beef to cool in the marinade.

Take beef out of the marinade and wrap in plastic wrap, twisting the ends closed to make a tight cylindrical shape. Refrigerate for at least 1 hour.

TO SERVE: Remove plastic wrap and cut beef into slices $\frac{1}{16}$-inch thick. Place beef slices on buttered bread and drizzle with the horseradish and mustard cream.

CREAM

¾ cup crème fraîche (page 136)

1 Tbsp store-bought creamed horseradish

1 Tbsp grainy mustard

MARINADE

1 Tbsp rice vinegar

1 Tbsp aged sherry vinegar

1 clove garlic, minced

3 Tbsp drained capers, rinsed and finely chopped

2 Tbsp minced shallot

2 Tbsp Dijon mustard

½ cup Italian (flat-leaf) parsley

1 Tbsp finely chopped fresh rosemary

2 Tbsp fresh thyme leaves

5 Tbsp extra-virgin olive oil

CARPACCIO

8 oz beef tenderloin

4 Tbsp canola oil

1 loaf pumpernickel bread, thinly sliced and lightly buttered

FRENCH ONION SOUP,

AU PIED DE COCHON

THOSE OF YOU who have been to Paris may have had a chance to try one of the most famous French onion soups in the world at Au Pied de Cochon. For me, it has become a ritual to go straight there for onion soup and a cleansing glass of Chablis. Since my cooking at Feenie's is all about fond food memories, this dish had to be on the menu. Bon appétit!

Speck is a delicious German ham, but you can also use prosciutto ends or a smoked ham hock. *Serves 4*

BOUQUET GARNI: Place all the ingredients on a 6-inch square of cheesecloth and tie closed with kitchen string.

SOUP: Place oil and half of the onions in a large, wide saucepan on medium-low heat. (A larger surface will help to cook and caramelize onions to get a rich flavour.) Slowly cook the onions for about 15 minutes, or until golden and translucent.

Add the other half of the onions, then increase the heat to medium-high and cook, stirring frequently, for 10 to 15 minutes, or until dark brown (be careful not to burn the onions). Season with salt and freshly ground white pepper. Stir in the flour until well mixed. Stir in wine and brandy. Cook for about 10 minutes, or until reduced by half.

Add chicken and veal stocks, speck and bouquet garni. Increase the heat to high and bring to a boil, then decrease to low and simmer for 45 minutes. Season to taste with salt and freshly ground white pepper. Remove from the stove. Take out and discard the bouquet garni and speck, then allow to cool.

TO SERVE: Reheat the soup. While the soup is reheating, preheat the broiler.

Pour the soup into four ovenproof French onion soup bowls until they are half full, then top each serving with 2 to 3 slices of baguette. Add more soup over baguette slices until the bowls are filled to the top.

Sprinkle ¼ cup cheese into each bowl. (This does not have to be neat and tidy. Your goal is a bubbling gooey topping, so if you want to add more cheese, go right ahead.) Place the soup bowls on a baking sheet and broil for 4 to 5 minutes, or until you get a nice crust on the cheese.

BOUQUET GARNI

1 bay leaf

2 sprigs fresh thyme

8 black peppercorns

2 stems fresh parsley

SOUP

2 Tbsp extra-virgin olive oil

6 Spanish onions, thinly sliced

2 Tbsp all-purpose flour

1 cup dry red wine

1 Tbsp brandy

1 quart dark chicken stock (page 132)

1 quart veal (page 134) or beef stock (page 133)

4 oz piece of speck, tied in cheesecloth

8 to 12 slices day-old baguette, 1-inch thick

1 cup grated Gruyère cheese

CORN AND CRAB CHOWDER

CHOWDER

1 lb crab shells

2 Tbsp olive oil

2 Tbsp extra-virgin olive oil

1 Spanish onion, thinly sliced

2 stalks celery,
coarsely chopped

1 large carrot,
coarsely chopped

5 ears corn, kernels
removed and cobs saved

2 quarts white chicken
stock (page 132)

2 cups whipping cream

6 basil leaves

Italian (flat-leaf) parsley,
roughly chopped, for garnish

FRITTERS

1 quart grapeseed oil

¾ cup corn kernels
(1 to 2 ears)

⅓ cup finely sliced basil leaves

⅓ cup all-purpose flour

⅓ tsp baking soda

1 cup milk

2 large eggs, separated

4 oz crabmeat

ONE COMBINATION that I really like is fresh sweet corn and crab. The flavours work so well together. This hearty soup makes a wonderful main course in the summer or a nice starter in cooler months. *Serves 6*

CHOWDER: Preheat the oven to 400°F. Place crab shells in a roasting pan and drizzle with olive oil. Place in the oven and roast for about 45 minutes, or until fragrant and light brown. Remove from the oven and allow to cool.

Heat extra-virgin olive oil in a saucepan on medium heat. Add onion, celery and carrot, then cook for 5 to 7 minutes, or until onions are translucent. Add corn kernels and cobs, then cook for 5 minutes.

Add stock and roasted crab shells, then simmer for 45 minutes. Stir in cream and basil. Bring just to a boil, then remove from the stove. Take out and discard corn cobs and crab shells, then allow to cool for 15 minutes.

Purée soup in a blender. Strain through a fine-mesh sieve, discard solids and allow to cool.

FRITTERS: Preheat oil to 375°F in a deep fryer. Combine corn, basil, flour and baking soda in a bowl.

In a separate bowl, mix milk and egg yolks. Add the milk mixture to the flour mixture, stirring well. Fold in crabmeat, then season with salt and freshly ground white pepper.

Beat egg whites in a bowl until stiff, then fold into the batter. Cover and refrigerate for 5 to 10 minutes.

Remove the batter from the refrigerator and spoon 1 Tbsp at a time into the hot oil, making sure the temperature is still 375°F. Cook 4 fritters at a time, making sure not to crowd them, for about 3 minutes. Take fritters out and drain on paper towels. Season with salt and freshly ground white pepper.

TO SERVE: Reheat the soup. Place 2 to 3 fritters in each of six warmed soup bowls and ladle chowder over them. Garnish with parsley.

also shown, in background:

CHUNKY TOMATO SOUP

CHILLED ASPARAGUS VELOUTÉ

WITH WATERCRESS CREAM

CREAM

½ bunch watercress, leaves only

½ cup crème fraîche (page 136)

VELOUTÉ

2 lbs asparagus

2 Tbsp olive oil

2 leeks, white parts only, sliced

1 quart vegetable stock

3 cups spinach

Extra-virgin olive oil, for garnish

THIS ELEGANT SOUP is quite simple to make and, if you are throwing a dinner party, to have ready ahead of time. Pair this recipe with our grilled lobster (page 50) and win the hearts of all your dinner guests! *Serves 4*

CREAM: Finely chop watercress leaves and place in a bowl. Add crème fraîche and mix well. Cover and refrigerate until needed.

VELOUTÉ: Cut off and discard woody bottoms of asparagus. Cut off the top inch of asparagus and set aside. Cut rest of stalks into slices ⅛-inch thick.

Fill a bowl with ice water and place a bowl on top of it. Heat oil in a large saucepan on medium-low heat. Add leeks and cook for about 4 minutes, or until soft. Add stock, increase the heat to high and bring to a boil. Add asparagus stalks and cook for about 5 minutes, or until tender. Add spinach and cook for 10 minutes, or until tender. Transfer the mixture to the bowl on top of the ice water and allow to cool.

Purée leek-asparagus mixture in small batches in a blender. Season with salt and freshly ground white pepper. Cover and refrigerate for at least 3 hours.

Fill a bowl with ice water. Bring a saucepan of salted water to a boil. Blanch asparagus tips by cooking in the boiling water for 3 minutes. Take asparagus tips out and immediately plunge them in the ice water. Drain and place on paper towels to dry.

TO SERVE: Pour the leek-asparagus mixture into four chilled bowls and top with a dollop of watercress cream. Garnish with asparagus tips and drizzle with a little oil.

CHUNKY
TOMATO SOUP

THERE ARE two types of soups: fine velvety puréed soups and chunky ones. You can enjoy this soup any time of the year and with the vegetables cut however you like them, chunky or fine. Tomato soup was one of my childhood favourites, and this recipe is all about the flavour of the tomatoes and the importance of the seasoning. This recipe makes about 3 quarts: if that's too much, you can freeze some for another day. *Serves 6 to 8*

BOUQUET GARNI: Place all the ingredients on a 6-inch square of cheesecloth and tie closed with kitchen string.

SOUP: Heat oil in a frying pan on medium heat. Add onion, fennel and leeks, then sauté for about 10 minutes, or until softened. Stir in saffron and wine, then increase the heat to high and bring to a boil.

Add tomatoes, stock and bouquet garni, then bring to a boil. Add potato and cook for about 10 minutes, until fork-tender. Take out and discard the bouquet garni. Season with salt.

TO SERVE: Pour soup into warmed bowls.

BOUQUET GARNI

3 sprigs fresh cilantro

3 sprigs fresh parsley

2 sprigs fresh thyme

3 cloves garlic

1 bay leaf

8 black peppercorns

1 Thai chili (page 24), crushed

1 thumbnail-size piece of ginger

SOUP

2 Tbsp canola oil

1 onion, ¼-inch dice

1 bulb fennel, ¼-inch dice

2 leeks, white and light green parts only, thumbnail-size chunks

Pinch of saffron

⅔ cup dry white wine

3 cans (each 8 oz) diced plum tomatoes

1½ quarts white chicken stock (page 132)

1 large Yukon Gold potato, thumbnail-size chunks

TOM YUM SOUP

À LA IRON CHEF

(page 24)

SOUP

4 Tbsp sunflower oil

3 Thai chilies
(page 24), crushed

4 cloves garlic, crushed

½ lb galangal, 1-inch lengths

½ lb ginger, 1-inch lengths

3 stalks lemon grass,
beaten, 1-inch lengths

⅓ leek, ½-inch slices

⅓ carrot, peeled,
½-inch slices

½ onion, 1-inch dice

6 kaffir lime leaves

1 sprig fresh basil

1 sprig fresh cilantro

4 Tbsp palm sugar

4 Tbsp tamarind paste

3 Tbsp + 1 tsp fish sauce

5 L water

¼ cup lime juice

CLARIFICATION

⅓ carrot

1 stalk celery

¼ onion

2 Tbsp ginger

¼ lb white fish (halibut,
snapper or sole)

¾ cup egg whites
(about 6 to 8 eggs)

THIS BROTH is a meeting of Japanese and West Coast cuisine. The delicate flavours of the crab and the sablefish demand that everything in the dish be as fresh as possible to let these flavours shine through. Although one *Iron Chef America* judge thought the sablefish was unnecessary in this soup, I still stick by our decision to include it because it adds such a wonderful, substantial element to an otherwise light meal. *Serves 4*

SOUP: Heat oil in a large pot on medium heat. Add Thai chilies and garlic, then sauté for 3 minutes, or until fragrant. Add galangal, ginger, lemon grass, leeks, carrots and onions, then cook for about 7 minutes, or until onions are translucent. Add the remaining ingredients, except for the lime juice. Increase the heat to high and bring to a boil, then decrease to low and simmer for 45 minutes. Allow to cool.

Strain soup through a fine-mesh sieve, and discard solids. Refrigerate until chilled, about 2 hours. Stir lime juice into chilled soup.

CLARIFICATION: Place carrot, celery, onion and ginger in a food processor and process until finely chopped. Add fish and pulse until the mixture becomes like a paste.

Beat egg whites in a bowl until frothy, then add the fish mixture and mix well until combined.

Place the chilled soup and the clarification mixture in a large pot on low heat, and stir well to combine. Cook, stirring occasionally, for the first 15 minutes. Continue cooking, without stirring, for about 1 hour, or until a "raft" of the clarification mixture floats to the top of the soup. (This "raft" will trap all of the impurities in the soup.) Simmer for another 10 minutes, then carefully poke a hole in the middle of the raft.

Line a fine-mesh sieve with cheesecloth, then place the sieve over a large bowl. Using a ladle, gently spoon the clarified stock into the sieve, being careful not to upset the raft. Strain the stock. Discard the raft and keep the stock hot.

TO SERVE: Preheat the oven to 400°F. Heat coconut and skim milks in a small pot on medium heat until warm (do not overheat the milk or it will not foam properly). Set warm milk aside.

Divide green onions, enoki and shiitake mushrooms, tomatoes and crabmeat among 4 bowls.

Rub sablefish with oil. Place in an ovenproof pan and roast in the oven for 5 to 7 minutes, or until done (flesh flakes easily with a fork).

Place a piece of sablefish in each bowl, then cover with 8 oz of soup.

Using an immersion blender, froth the milk mixture. Spoon 3 Tbsp froth on top of the soup in each bowl. Garnish each serving with 2 Thai basil leaves and 2 cilantro leaves.

GARNISH

5 Tbsp coconut milk

1 cup skim milk

2 green onions, finely sliced

1 bunch enoki mushrooms, trimmed, 1-inch lengths

2 shiitake mushrooms, stems removed and thinly sliced

2 roma tomatoes, peeled, seeded and ¼-inch dice

¼ lb crab leg meat, cooked

4 pieces sablefish (each 2½ oz)

1 Tbsp sunflower oil

8 Thai basil leaves

8 cilantro leaves

PORTOBELLO MUSHROOM
AND PROSCIUTTO SALAD

VINAIGRETTE

¼ cup balsamic vinegar

1 Tbsp Dijon mustard

½ cup extra-virgin olive oil

SALAD

4 large portobello
mushrooms, destemmed

½ cup extra-virgin olive oil

1 tsp salt

1 clove garlic, thinly sliced

8 sprigs fresh thyme

4 cups arugula

5 oz prosciutto, thinly sliced

½ cup freshly grated Parmesan

ONE OF THE THINGS I love about this salad is how meaty portobellos are. If you are trying to cut back on the meat in your diet, these hearty fungi are the way to go! *Serves 4*

VINAIGRETTE: Whisk together balsamic vinegar and mustard in a small bowl. Slowly add oil, whisking all the while. Season with salt and freshly ground white pepper. Cover and refrigerate until needed.

SALAD: Preheat the oven to 450°F. Use the back of a spoon to carefully scrape out and discard the gills from the mushroom caps. Drizzle ¼ cup of the oil over a small roasting pan, then sprinkle with ½ tsp of the salt. Place mushroom caps, cleaned side up, in the pan. Drizzle with the remaining olive oil and salt.

Place 2 to 3 slices of garlic and 2 sprigs of thyme on each mushroom. Season with freshly ground white pepper. Place in the oven and roast for 10 minutes, or until mushrooms are soft. Remove from the oven and allow to cool. Discard garlic and thyme.

Toss together arugula and vinaigrette in a large bowl. Season with salt and freshly ground white pepper.

TO SERVE: Place a mushroom on each of four dinner plates and top with prosciutto. Top with arugula and sprinkle with Parmesan.

TOMATO AND BUFFALO
MOZZARELLA SALAD

THIS IS a classic Italian salad and probably one of the easiest to make. The secret is to use the best ingredients: ripe organic tomatoes and good-quality buffalo mozzarella, balsamic vinegar and extra-virgin olive oil. The buffalo mozzarella has a terrific flavour, but if you can't get it, substitute 6 large bocconcini. *Serves 4*

1 cup balsamic vinegar

6 large tomatoes, ½-inch slices

2 large buffalo mozzarella, ½-inch slices

2 Tbsp basil oil (page 137)

4 fresh basil leaves, for garnish

Place balsamic vinegar in a large saucepan on medium-low heat and cook for about 1 hour, or until reduced by half.

On a large platter, arrange alternate slices of tomato and mozzarella. Sprinkle with coarse salt and freshly ground white pepper.

TO SERVE: Whisk together reduced balsamic vinegar with basil oil in a small bowl. Drizzle over salad and garnish with fresh basil leaves.

BLUE CHEESE AND
APPLE COLESLAW

I SOMETIMES FEEL that I could add blue cheese to any salad. This recipe is a wonderful play of soft and crunchy textures and both tangy and sweet flavours that work perfectly together. A big bowl of this coleslaw is a perfect light meal on hot summer evenings. *Serves 6*

Mix together mayonnaise and sour cream in a large bowl. Stir in lemon juice, horseradish, sugar and salt. Add endives, apples, green onions and blue cheese, then toss together. Cover and refrigerate for least 30 minutes to allow flavours to develop before serving.

TO SERVE: Divide salad among six chilled plates. Garnish with endive leaves.

½ cup mayonnaise (page 136)

½ cup sour cream

2 Tbsp lemon juice

3 Tbsp drained store-bought horseradish

1 tsp sugar

1 tsp salt

4 endives, finely shredded

1 cup diced (½ inch) Granny Smith or Braeburn apples

4 green onions, chopped

½ cup blue cheese (Roquefort, Stilton or Bresse blue), crumbled

Belgian endive leaves, for garnish

FEENIE'S
CAESAR SALAD

PANCETTA CRISPS

4 slices pancetta or honey-smoked bacon

CROUTONS

1 Tbsp melted unsalted butter

1 tsp red chili flakes

1 clove garlic, minced

8 slices French baguette, ¼-inch thick

DRESSING

5 fillets anchovies, fresh or canned

2 eggs

½ lemon, juice only

3 cloves garlic, minced

1 Tbsp grated Parmesan

1 Tbsp Dijon mustard

1 Tbsp 2% yogurt

1 cup extra-virgin olive oil

SALAD

1 head iceberg lettuce

1 lemon, in peeled segments

GARNISH

½ cup grated or shaved Parmesan

4 tsp extra-virgin olive oil

EVERYONE HAS their own take on the classic Caesar salad. Some people love a tart version with lots of lemon. Others like plenty of garlic and Parmesan. Ours has a little bit of everything. Traditionally, this dish is made with romaine lettuce, but I prefer iceberg, a very familiar staple from my childhood. Its crispness and high water content balance the saltiness of the dressing. *Serves 4*

PANCETTA CRISPS: Preheat the oven to 375°F. Place pancetta on a baking sheet and bake in the oven for 7 to 10 minutes, or until crispy. Remove from the oven and allow to cool. Leave the oven on for the croutons.

CROUTONS: Combine melted butter, chili flakes and garlic in a small bowl. Place baguette slices on a baking sheet and brush evenly with the butter mixture. Toast in the oven for 6 to 8 minutes, or until dry and crisp. Remove from the oven, then season with salt and freshly ground white pepper.

DRESSING: Place all the ingredients, except for the oil, in a blender. Purée until smooth. With the motor running, slowly add oil. Season with salt and freshly ground white pepper.

SALAD: Cut lettuce in 8 equal portions, but leave leaves attached to the core. Toss together iceberg lettuce and ¾ cup of the dressing in a large bowl. Season with salt and freshly ground white pepper. Add lemon segments and toss vigorously.

TO SERVE: Divide salad among four chilled plates and drizzle with any remaining dressing (optional). Crumble pancetta over the salads, then sprinkle them with Parmesan and drizzle with extra-virgin olive oil. Top each serving with 2 croutons.

NEW POTATO SALAD

WITH LEMON-THYME CRÈME FRAÎCHE

WHEN I lived in Sweden many years ago, I used to love when the new potatoes came into season in the spring. There is nothing more simple or delicious than crisp little potatoes and lots of sweet butter. Adding the thyme and crème fraîche just gives this classic dish a little lift, but really the potato is still the star of the show. *Serves 4*

CRÈME FRAÎCHE: Combine all the ingredients in a small bowl. Mix well. Season with salt and freshly ground white pepper.

SALAD: Place new potatoes in a saucepan of salted water on medium-high heat. Bring to a gentle boil and cook for 15 to 20 minutes, or until fork-tender. Drain potatoes and allow to cool.

Fill a bowl with ice water. Bring a saucepan of salted water to a boil on high heat. Blanch green beans by cooking in the boiling water for 2 to 3 minutes, depending on the thickness, until al dente. Do not overcook, as you want to retain the colour and crunchy texture. Take green beans out and immediately plunge them in the ice water. Drain green beans. Repeat the process for wax beans.

TO SERVE: If new potatoes are large, cut them in half. Cut green beans and wax beans into lengths of 1½ to 2 inches.

Place potatoes, green beans and wax beans in a large bowl and toss gently with lemon-thyme crème fraîche. Season with fleur de sel and freshly ground white pepper.

CRÈME FRAÎCHE

2 lemons, fine zest only

½ lemon, juice only

1 cup crème fraîche (page 136)

3 tsp fresh thyme leaves

SALAD

8 oz new potatoes

4 oz thin green beans

4 oz thin wax beans

Fleur de sel

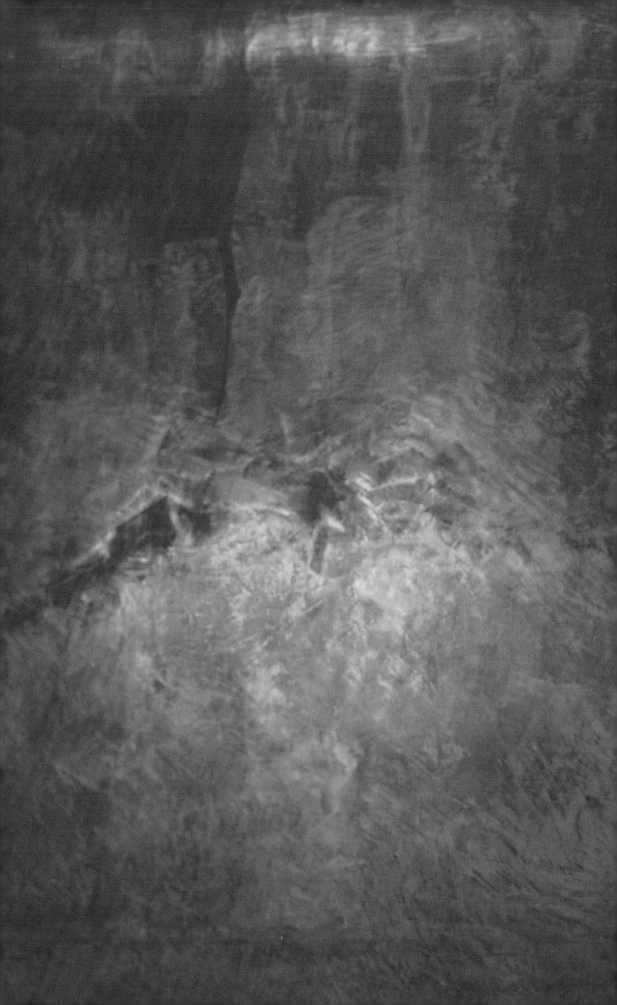

FEENIE'S SIDE DISHES

BROCCOLI AND
CHORIZO GRATIN

BÉCHAMEL SAUCE

¼ cup butter

¼ cup flour

1 cup whipping cream

3 cups milk

¼ onion, sliced

2 cloves

1 bay leaf

1 sprig fresh thyme

Pinch of nutmeg

GRATIN

4 heads broccoli, in florets

2 Tbsp extra-virgin olive oil

8 oz chorizo, ¼-inch slices

1 cup grated Parmesan cheese

1 cup grated Gruyère cheese

TRAVELLING TO SPAIN has opened my eyes to a whole array of tapas. That's why I love to cook side dishes with the focus on vegetables. In this dish, we combine a vegetable with meat: broccoli and chorizo sausage. *Serves 6*

BÉCHAMEL SAUCE: Melt butter in a saucepan on low heat, then slowly stir in flour a little at a time until it is all incorporated. Cook for 2 to 3 minutes. Remove from the stove and, while the mixture is still warm, vigorously stir in cream.

Return the pot to the stove on medium heat, then add milk, 1 cup at a time, stirring well. Add onion, cloves, bay leaf, thyme and nutmeg. Continue to stir while bringing the mixture to a simmer. When it has simmered for 10 minutes and thickened, remove from the stove. Season to taste with salt and freshly ground white pepper. Strain through a fine-mesh sieve and discard the solids. Keep the sauce warm.

GRATIN: Preheat the broiler. Fill a bowl with ice water. Bring a saucepan of salted water to a boil. Blanch broccoli by cooking in the boiling water for 3 minutes. Take broccoli out and immediately plunge into the ice water. Drain broccoli.

Heat oil in a large frying pan. Add chorizo and sauté for about 8 minutes, or until golden brown. Add warm béchamel sauce and broccoli. Toss gently to coat broccoli and chorizo evenly with the sauce, then transfer the mixture to a casserole dish. Top with Parmesan and Gruyère, then place under the broiler until the top is brown and bubbling. Remove from the broiler and serve.

CREAMED SPINACH

THIS IS probably one of my favourite side dishes of all time. When I think of meat, I think of creamed spinach. This is a side dish that you really could eat on its own and forget everything else. The key to making it is to remove as much water as you can from the cooked spinach. *Serves 4*

2 cups whipping cream

1 shallot, ¼-inch dice

2 cloves garlic, chopped

1 sprig fresh thyme

3½ lbs spinach leaves

4 Tbsp grated Parmesan

Combine cream, shallot, garlic and thyme in a small saucepan on medium heat. Bring to a simmer, then cook for about 10 minutes, until reduced by half. Strain through a fine-mesh sieve and discard the solids.

Fill a bowl with ice water. Bring a large saucepan of salted water to a boil. Blanch spinach by cooking in the boiling water for no more than 20 seconds. Take spinach out and immediately plunge it into the ice water. Drain spinach and squeeze out as much water as possible.

Place the cream mixture and spinach in a food processor and process until well combined. Season with salt and freshly ground white pepper.

Reheat creamed spinach in a saucepan on medium heat. If there is any water left in the mixture, slowly increase the heat until most of the water has evaporated. Stir in Parmesan. Remove from the stove and transfer to a serving dish.

SPICY
GREEN BEANS

1 cup green beans, trimmed
4 Tbsp sunflower oil
4 tsp finely chopped anchovies
2 tsp chopped garlic
5 tsp sambal oelek

THIS DISH combines the crisp freshness of green beans, the saltiness of anchovies and the spiciness of sambal oelek, an Indonesian chili-garlic sauce. The recipe was inspired by the Szechwan green beans served at the excellent Chinese restaurants here in Vancouver. The best time to make this is in spring and summer, when green beans are in season. You can also use wax beans instead. *Serves 4*

Fill a bowl with ice water. Bring a saucepan of generously salted water to a boil. Blanch green beans by cooking them in the boiling water for 2 to 3 minutes. Take green beans out and immediately plunge them into the ice water. Drain green beans.

Heat oil in a large frying pan on medium heat. Add anchovies and garlic, then sauté for 30 seconds. Add sambal oelek and green beans, tossing the beans until they are evenly coated, then cook for 2 minutes. Season with salt and freshly ground white pepper. Remove from the stove and transfer to a serving dish.

also shown, in background:
WINE-BRAISED RED CABBAGE

WINE-BRAISED RED CABBAGE, ONION AND APPLE

SPICE SACHET

10 juniper berries, crushed

5 allspice, crushed

2 bay leaves

1 bunch fresh thyme

RED CABBAGE,
ONION AND APPLE

5 Tbsp rendered
duck fat (page 135)

8 oz double-smoked
bacon, in thin strips

2 red cabbages, cored and
thinly sliced

4 onions, thinly sliced

5 Granny Smith apples,
peeled, cored and ½-inch dice

4 cloves garlic, finely chopped

1 cup apple juice

1 cup dry white wine

½ cup fresh lemon juice

2 tsp freshly ground cinnamon

1 tsp freshly ground nutmeg

I F YOU ARE a fan of cabbage like me, this is the recipe for you. The important ingredients are the bacon and duck fat. Most of the other ingredients such as the juniper berries and cinnamon are classic, but the addition of apples puts it over the top. This is one of the best winter side dishes ever. Try it with salmon, halibut, pork or sausages (my personal favourite is bratwurst). *Serves 6*

SPICE SACHET: Place all the ingredients on a 6-inch square of cheesecloth and tie closed with kitchen string.

CABBAGE, ONION AND APPLE: Place duck fat and bacon in a large saucepan on medium heat, then cook for about 5 minutes, or until bacon is limp (do not brown). Add cabbages, onions, apples and garlic, then cook for about 10 minutes, or until cabbage is slightly wilted.

Add the remaining ingredients and the spice sachet, then cook for 15 to 20 minutes, or until cabbage is tender but still has a bit of a bite. Season to taste with salt and freshly ground white pepper. Remove from the stove, discard sachet and transfer to a serving dish.

GLAZED
NEW POTATOES

NEW POTATOES are available from early spring through early summer, but any potatoes will work nicely (you will need to quarter them after cooking). Be sure to use a large casserole dish and make sure the potatoes are constantly covered with stock so they don't dry out. You will end up with a sauce but the glaze also should be soaked into the potatoes.
Serves 4

Fill a bowl with ice water. Bring a saucepan of salted water to a boil. Blanch leeks by cooking in the boiling water for 30 seconds. Take leeks out and immediately plunge them into the ice water.

Preheat the oven to 375°F. Place potatoes, salt, stock, butter, garlic and thyme in a large casserole dish. Cover with a lid and cook on medium heat for about 10 minutes, or until potatoes are fork-tender. Take potatoes out of the dish and set aside, keeping them warm.

Strain the cooking liquid through a fine-mesh sieve into a large nonstick pan on medium heat, then cook for about 10 minutes, or until reduced to a syrup.

Increase the heat to high, then add potatoes, toss gently to coat evenly and cook for about 5 minutes, or until lightly glazed. Add leeks and toss gently. Season with salt and freshly ground white pepper. Remove from the stove and transfer to a serving dish.

4 baby leeks or green onion, 1-inch lengths

12 oz assorted new potatoes, unpeeled

½ tsp sea salt

1½ cups white chicken stock (page 132)

3 Tbsp unsalted butter

1 clove garlic

3 sprigs fresh thyme

SPRING VEGETABLE RAGOUT

WITH YUZU MOUSSELINE

RAGOUT

4 to 5 stalks green
asparagus, peeled

4 to 5 stalks white
asparagus, peeled

¼ cup pearl onions

½ cup baby carrots,
peeled and trimmed

½ cup baby turnips,
peeled and trimmed

½ cup green beans, trimmed

2 Tbsp butter

2 Tbsp olive oil

⅓ cup vegetable
stock (page 135)

MOUSSELINE

1 egg yolk

2 Tbsp sake

¼ cup yuzu juice

½ cup clarified butter

2 Tbsp thawed and
chopped frozen yuzu peel

¼ cup whipping cream,
whipped to soft peaks

THIS RAGOUT is beautiful to look at, with the combination of green and white asparagus and orange carrots. I've added a citrus flavour that is unusual—yuzu, a Japanese fruit that looks like a mini lime but has a distinctive flavour. You can get bottled yuzu juice and frozen peel in Japanese specialty stores. *Serves 4*

RAGOUT: Cut off and discard woody bottoms of green and white asparagus. Cut into 1½-inch lengths.

Fill a bowl with ice water. Bring a saucepan of salted water to a boil. Blanch green asparagus by cooking in the boiling water for 2 to 3 minutes. Take asparagus out and immediately plunge into the ice water.

Repeat the blanching process, a vegetable at a time, for white asparagus (2 to 3 minutes), pearl onions (5 minutes, peel them after blanching), carrots (5 to 7 minutes), turnips (5 to 7 minutes) and green beans (5 to 7 minutes).

Heat butter and oil in a large frying pan on medium heat. Add all vegetables and sauté for 2 minutes. Add stock and cook for 5 to 7 minutes, or until vegetables are heated through and nicely glazed. Season with salt and freshly ground white pepper. Remove from the stove and transfer to a serving dish.

MOUSSELINE: Combine egg yolk, sake and yuzu juice in a heatproof bowl (or in the top of a double boiler) set over barely simmering water on medium heat. Whisk for about 3 minutes, or until the mixture is pale and thick. Whisking constantly, slowly drizzle in butter until the mixture is thick. Fold in yuzu peel and whipped cream.

Top the ragout with the yuzu mousseline and serve.

CELERIAC AND POTATO PAVÉ

THERE ARE PAVÉS with potatoes, better known as scalloped potatoes, but try using celeriac, one of my favourite vegetables. You can make this without worrying too much about overcooking it, because you want it to be fork-tender. This is a perfect main dish if you are vegetarian, and it is also a perfect side dish for roast lamb, pork, chicken or steak. *Serves 6*

2 lbs celeriac, thinly sliced

3 large Yukon Gold potatoes, thinly sliced

1 quart whipping cream

½ lb blue cheese, crumbled

Preheat the oven to 400°F. Grease an ovenproof pan 11 × 7 inches. Arrange alternate layers of celeriac and potato slices in the pan, seasoning each layer with salt and freshly ground white pepper. Pour cream over top. Bake in the oven for 40 to 50 minutes, until the potatoes are nearly cooked.

Remove the pan from the oven and sprinkle blue cheese on top. Return to the oven and bake for 15 to 20 minutes, or until the top is golden brown and potatoes are fork-tender.

Remove from the oven and serve.

BACON AND CHILI CORNBREAD

THERE IS nothing better than eating this cornbread with lots of butter soon after it comes out of the oven. What makes this recipe luxurious is the addition of the bacon. *Makes 12*

Preheat the oven to 350°F. Lightly grease a muffin tin.

Place jalapeño peppers on a baking sheet and roast in the oven for 20 minutes, or until their skins start to darken. Leave the oven on, but transfer the peppers to a bowl and cover it with plastic wrap for 10 minutes, to help loosen the skins to make them easier to peel. Peel, deseed and cut into ⅛-inch dice.

Sauté bacon in a frying pan on medium-high heat for about 5 minutes, or until crispy. Take bacon out of the pan and discard the fat. Drain bacon on paper towels.

Combine eggs, corn, sour cream and oil in a large bowl. In another large bowl, combine flour, cornmeal, sugar, baking powder and salt. Add the flour mixture all at once to the corn mixture, then mix until just combined. Stir in jalapeños, bacon, parsley and green onions.

Pour the batter into the prepared muffin tin and bake in the oven for 30 to 40 minutes, or until golden brown. Remove from the oven and allow to rest for 10 minutes before taking cornbread out of the muffin tin.

6 jalapeño peppers

3 slices bacon, ¼-inch dice

2 eggs

1 cup canned creamed corn

1 cup sour cream

¼ cup grapeseed or corn oil

½ cup all-purpose flour

½ cup yellow cornmeal

⅓ cup sugar

2 Tbsp baking powder

1 tsp salt

2 Tbsp chopped parsley

¼ cup chopped green onions

SOFT
POLENTA

1 quart whipping cream

3 cups white chicken stock (page 132)

1 cup fine cornmeal

1 Tbsp butter

2 Tbsp grated Parmesan

FOR THOSE of you who enjoy the wonderful creamy texture of perfect mashed potatoes or risotto, I present our version of polenta. The cheese in this dish is positively sensational and helps make this side dish a welcome accompaniment for so many dishes. It is perfect with any red meat or poultry, and even meatier varieties of fish. *Serves 4*

Line a baking sheet with parchment paper. Combine cream and 2 cups of the stock in a saucepan on medium heat, then bring to a boil. Season with salt and freshly ground white pepper.

Whisking vigorously all the while, slowly add cornmeal and cook for about 10 minutes, or until thickened and the liquid is absorbed. Season with salt and freshly ground white pepper, then spread on the prepared baking sheet to cool.

Just before serving, place 2 Tbsp of the polenta and the remaining stock in a saucepan on medium heat, and whisk together. Add butter and Parmesan. Whisk in the remaining polenta a little at a time, until well mixed and heated through. Remove from the stove and transfer to a serving dish.

To MAKE orange gnocchi, blanch the zest of 1 orange for 30 seconds in boiling water, drain, then add together with the flour. *Serves 4 to 6*

2 large Yukon Gold potatoes (about 1 lb), unpeeled

1 large egg yolk

¼ to 1 cup all-purpose flour

Place potatoes in a saucepan, cover with water and bring to a boil on high heat. Simmer for about 20 minutes, or until fork-tender. Drain potatoes and allow to cool, then slip off the skins.

Press potatoes through a ricer or coarsely grate them into a large bowl. Add yolk and mix with a wooden spoon until well blended.

Place the mixture on a lightly floured surface, then knead in a small amount of flour at a time, until the dough is smooth but still slightly sticky. Season with salt and freshly ground white pepper.

Bring a small saucepan of salted water to a boil on high heat. Add a small piece of the dough. If it floats to the surface, the dough is fine. If it falls apart, knead in a little more flour and test again.

Form the dough into a large log, then cut into 4 sections. Roll each section into a log ½ inch in diameter. Cut into lengths of ½ inch and delicately indent each piece by pinching it lightly in the middle. Dust well with flour.

Spread gnocchi on a parchment-lined baking sheet and freeze. Place in resealable bags until needed. Will keep in the freezer for 2 months.

To cook, bring a saucepan of salted water to a boil on high heat. Add gnocchi and cook for 2 to 3 minutes, or until they begin to float to the surface. As they surface, remove with a slotted spoon and drain well. They can be tossed in a heated sauce before serving.

CHEESES AND
CHARCUTERIES

WHEN I WAS in Rome in the early nineties, I was sitting in a wine bar in rapt attention with a list of wines by the glass that topped 100 varieties. After a glass of super Tuscan wine and some beautiful prosciutto and fontina, I fell in love with this style of dining. This is where the inspiration for our cheese and charcuterie plates came from.

Cheese and charcuterie plates are a wonderful way to eat because they are so versatile. What goes on to these platters is totally up to you, so they are a perfect addition to any party menu, especially if you want to serve your guests light nibbles but not a full meal. Try to choose meats and cheeses with a variety of flavours, textures, colours and degrees of spiciness. (If you are unsure about what cheeses or meats to put together, visit your local specialty shop and ask for some guidance.) Offering your guests an assortment that ranges from the familiar to the exotic is always the best way to go.

For cheese boards, we start with one soft cheese, such as a ripe brie; one sharply flavoured, hard cheese, such as an aged cheddar; perhaps a lovely floral, mild cheese like the Brie de Meaux from France; a plain or flavoured goat cheese and even some chunks of aged Parmesan. A beautiful blue is also a great addition.

For charcuterie boards, we look for contrasting meats to add variety and appeal. Spicy chorizo, rich smoked duck salami, chewy air-dried beef and a creamy pâté are always a good start.

Serve the platters with a few olives, some of your favourite pickles and slices of hearty breads. This is truly a meal in itself and, paired with a glass of wine, it is "peasant dining" at its finest.

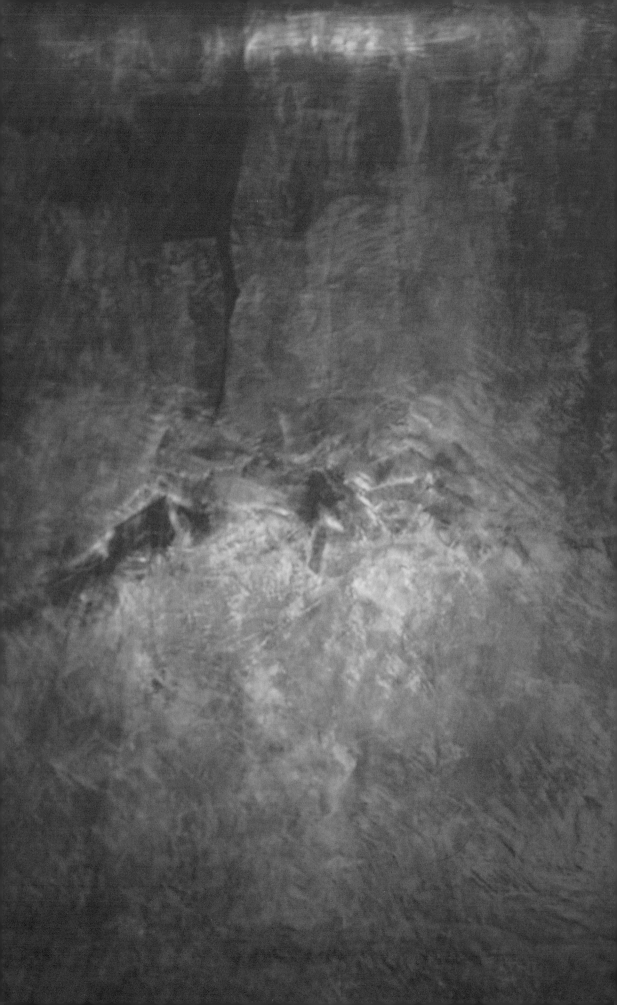

FEENIE'S DESSERTS

APPLE GALETTE

ICE CREAM

1 cup + 2 Tbsp sugar

3 cups whipping cream

1 cup milk

2 vanilla beans,
pulp only (page 10)

12 egg yolks

FRANGIPANE

⅓ cup butter

¼ cup sugar

1 cup ground blanched
almonds

2 Tbsp all-purpose flour

2 eggs

CARAMEL SAUCE

½ cup water

2 cups sugar

2 tsp corn syrup

1½ cups whipping cream

1 cup butter

THIS APPLE GALETTE was one of the very first items I put on the menu at Lumière. It moved from there to the tasting bar and is now a permanent fixture at Feenie's. I have tried to take it off the menu several times, but people have demanded it be put back on. Have extra caramel sauce on hand for a real treat! *Serves 6 to 8*

ICE CREAM: Place half of the sugar in the bottom of a saucepan, then add cream, milk and vanilla. Cook on medium heat until it comes just to a boil, then remove from the stove.

Whisk together egg yolks and the remaining sugar in a bowl. Temper the egg mixture (so that it doesn't curdle) by whisking in ¼ cup of the warm cream mixture. Slowly whisk in the remaining warm cream mixture.

Transfer the mixture to a saucepan on medium heat and bring to 175°F (80 to 82°C) on a digital instant-read thermometer. Stir constantly and keep scraping the bottom of the pot with a spatula.

Fill a bowl with ice water and place another bowl on top of it. Strain the mixture through a fine-mesh sieve into the bowl on top of the ice water, then stir until completely cool. Cover and refrigerate overnight. Place in an ice-cream maker and process according to the manufacturer's instructions. Freeze until needed.

FRANGIPANE: Cream together butter and sugar in a kitchen mixer with a paddle attachment. Mix in ground almonds and flour. Add eggs one at a time, mixing well after each one. Cover and refrigerate; will keep for up to a week.

CARAMEL SAUCE: Place water in a saucepan, then add sugar and corn syrup. Cook on high heat, brushing the sides of the pot with water to keep sugar from crystallizing. Cook for 10 to 15 minutes, or until the mixture turns a dark amber colour. Stir in cream carefully, as it may splatter a bit.

Decrease the heat to low and add butter, whisking until melted and completely mixed. Increase the heat to high and bring back just to a boil, then remove from the stove.

Fill a bowl with ice water and place another bowl on top of it. Strain the mixture through a fine-mesh sieve into the bowl on top of the ice water and allow to cool.

APPLE GALETTE: Preheat the oven to 400°F. Line a baking sheet with parchment paper. Combine sugar and cinnamon in a small bowl.

Roll out puff pastry on a lightly floured board to a thickness of ⅛ inch. Cut out 6 to 8 rounds, using a 6-inch diameter cutter. Place pastry rounds on the prepared baking sheet.

Spread equal amounts of the frangipane in the centre of each pastry round. Arrange apple slices in a spiral pattern on top of the frangipane. Brush apples with melted butter, then sprinkle with the cinnamon mixture.

Refrigerate the galettes for 15 minutes. Bake in the oven for 12 to 15 minutes, or until pastry is puffed and the bottoms are golden.

TO SERVE: If the caramel sauce is not at room temperature, warm it a little in the microwave on high at 15-second intervals (should be warm, not hot). Place a galette in the centre of each of 6 to 8 plates, and surround each with a ribbon of caramel sauce. Dust the top of each galette with icing sugar and top with a scoop of vanilla ice cream.

APPLE GALETTE

1 cup sugar

2 to 3 Tbsp ground cinnamon

1 lb frozen puff pastry, thawed

4 to 5 Granny Smith apples, peeled, cored and thinly sliced

¼ cup melted butter

Icing sugar, for garnish

CHERRY CHOCOLATE CLAFOUTIS

ONE OF the most fabulous cherry desserts is a clafoutis. It's easy to make, and we've given this recipe an extra edge by adding chocolate. Use your favourite kind of cherry (we like Bing). Be sure to serve the clafoutis warm. *Serves 6 to 8*

Preheat the oven to 350°F. Butter and lightly sugar six to eight shallow ramekins or crème brûlée dishes, 6 inches in diameter. Place cherries and Kirsch in a bowl.

Place eggs, egg yolks and sugar in a kitchen mixer with a whisk attachment and mix until smooth. Mix in melted chocolate. Slowly add and mix in milk and cream. Fold ground almonds, flour, cocoa and vanilla into the batter.

Divide cherries and Kirsch among the ramekins, then add chocolate pieces. Fill ramekins to the top with batter (about ¼ cup per dish). Bake in the oven for about 15 minutes, or until cake is done (a toothpick inserted into the centre comes out clean).

TO SERVE: Place each ramekin on a plate. Garnish each clafoutis with a dollop of whipped cream.

1 cup pitted and quartered cherries

1 Tbsp Kirsch

2 eggs

2 egg yolks

⅓ cup sugar

3 oz 66% dark or bittersweet chocolate, melted

1 cup milk

1 cup whipping cream

1 cup ground almonds

3 Tbsp all-purpose flour

1 Tbsp cocoa powder

2 vanilla beans, pulp only (page 10)

3 oz 66% dark or bittersweet chocolate, chopped

Whipped cream, for garnish

STRAWBERRY RHUBARB CRISP

WITH PECAN TOPPING, BLACKBERRY COMPOTE AND LEMON-BASIL ICE CREAM

ICE CREAM

1 cup packed fresh basil leaves

2 Tbsp simple syrup (page 137)

½ cup sugar

1½ cups milk

½ cup whipping cream

1 tsp vanilla extract

3 lemons, zest only

Pinch of salt

6 egg yolks

TOPPING

½ cup all-purpose flour

½ cup quick oats

½ cup ground pecans

½ cup packed brown sugar

¾ cup butter, cold,
in small pieces

LATE SPRING, when both strawberries and rhubarb are in season, is the time to make this crisp. The sweetness of the strawberries and the tartness of the rhubarb are a classic combination. The lemon-basil ice cream takes this dish over the top. *Makes 6 to 8 ramekins (or 1 casserole dish, but will need to be baked longer)*

ICE CREAM: Fill a bowl with ice water. Bring a saucepan of water to a boil. Blanch basil leaves by placing them in the boiling water for 20 seconds. Take basil leaves out and immediately plunge them into the ice water. When cool, drain well. Place basil and simple syrup in a blender and purée.

Place half of the sugar in the bottom of a saucepan, then add milk, cream, vanilla, lemon zest and salt. Cook on medium heat until it just comes to a boil, then remove from the stove.

Whisk together egg yolks and the remaining sugar in a bowl. Temper the egg mixture (so that it doesn't curdle) by whisking in ¼ cup of the warm milk mixture. Slowly whisk in the remaining warm milk mixture.

Transfer the mixture to a saucepan on medium heat and bring to 175°F (80 to 82°C) on a digital instant-read thermometer. Stir constantly and keep scraping the bottom of the pot with a spatula.

Fill a bowl with ice water and place another bowl on top of it. Pour the mixture into the bowl on top of the ice water and stir until completely cool. Add the basil purée and mix well. Cover and refrigerate overnight. Strain through a fine-mesh sieve. Place in an ice-cream maker and process according to the manufacturer's instructions. Freeze until needed.

TOPPING: Place all the ingredients in a large bowl. Use your hands to crumble butter into the dry ingredients. Continue mixing until you have a crumbly dough that has small chunks of butter about the size of a pea. Cover and refrigerate until needed.

COMPOTE: Toss 1 cup of the blackberries with sugar in a bowl, and let sit for 10 minutes. Place the berry mixture and simple syrup in a blender and puree. Strain through a fine-mesh sieve into a bowl. Add the remaining blackberries and toss gently to coat evenly.

LEMON CONFIT: Slice lemon thinly into rounds. Remove and discard any seeds. Place lemon slices in a small saucepan and cover with simple syrup. Lay a round piece of parchment paper on top of lemon and syrup. Cook on low heat for about an hour. Remove the parchment, then cook for about 10 minutes, or until syrup thickens. Remove from the heat and allow to cool. Cover and refrigerate until needed.

FILLING: Preheat the oven to 375°F. Butter the ramekins.

Place all the ingredients in a large bowl and toss together. Pour into the prepared ramekins, then cover with topping. Bake in the oven for 20 to 30 minutes, or until juices bubble at the edges of the ramekins.

TO SERVE: Place the ramekins on large plates. Place 2 Tbsp of the blackberry compote and 1 Tbsp of the lemon confit on each plate beside the ramekins. Place a scoop of the ice cream on top of the crisp.

COMPOTE

3 cups blackberries

2 Tbsp sugar

2 Tbsp simple syrup

LEMON CONFIT

1 lemon

2 cups simple syrup

FILLING

4 cups chopped rhubarb

3 cups chopped strawberries

2 Tbsp cornstarch

2 cups sugar

2 tsp vanilla extract

1 vanilla bean,
pulp only (page 10)

BANANA CREAM PIE

WITH ALMOND SHORTCRUST

SHORTCRUST

1 cup butter

¾ cup icing sugar

2 eggs

1 lemon, zest only

1 tsp bitter almond flavouring

1 tsp vanilla extract

3 cups all-purpose flour

1¼ cups ground
blanched almonds

Pinch of salt

CUSTARD

2½ cups whipping cream

1 cup milk

1 vanilla bean, pulp
only (page 10)

1½ cups sugar

2 eggs

3 egg yolks

1 cup cornstarch

Dark rum to taste

CHANTILLY CREAM

2 cups whipping cream

¼ cup icing sugar

2 tsp vanilla extract

FILLING

4 to 5 ripe bananas, sliced

2 Tbsp lemon juice, strained

3 oz 66% dark or bittersweet
chocolate, melted

Shaved 66% dark
chocolate, for garnish

IN MY COOKING at Lumière, I strive for the ultimate dinner. What I love about Feenie's is being able to have a bit more fun by preparing something like a simple banana cream pie. My mom used to make it when I was little, and the taste of bananas and whipped cream takes me right back. *Makes a 10-inch pie*

SHORTCRUST: Cream together butter and icing sugar in a kitchen mixer with a paddle attachment. Mix in eggs, lemon zest, bitter almond and vanilla.

Combine flour, ground almonds and salt in a bowl. Add the flour mixture all at once to the butter mixture, then mix well. Form the dough into ball, wrap in plastic wrap and refrigerate for at least 4 hours.

Preheat the oven to 350°F. Roll out the dough on a lightly floured surface to a thickness of ⅛ inch. Fit the dough into the pie plate.

Cut a square of aluminum foil, 13 by 13 inches, and use it to line the pie shell. Add dried beans, about 2 cups, to prevent bubbles from forming when you bake the pie shell. (Do not discard the dried beans, as they can be used repeatedly.)

Bake the pie shell in the oven for 15 to 20 minutes, or until slightly golden. Remove from the oven, remove the beans and foil, then allow to cool.

CUSTARD: Place cream, milk, vanilla and half of the sugar in a saucepan on high heat. Bring just to a boil, then remove from the stove.

Whisk together eggs, egg yolks, cornstarch and the remaining sugar in a large bowl. Temper the egg mixture (so that it doesn't curdle) by whisking in ¼ cup of the warm cream mixture. Gradually whisk in the rest of the warm cream mixture. Transfer the mixture to a saucepan on low heat and cook for 5 to 7 minutes, or until thickened and glossy.

Fill a bowl with ice water and place another bowl on top of it. Strain the mixture through a fine-mesh sieve into the bowl on top of the ice water. Allow to cool to room temperature.

Place a sheet of plastic wrap directly on the surface of the custard so that a skin does not form. Allow to cool, then stir in rum.

CHANTILLY CREAM: Combine cream, icing sugar and vanilla in a bowl. Whip until stiff (be careful not to overwhip).

FILLING: Toss together banana slices and lemon juice in a bowl. Brush the inside of the cooled pie shell with melted chocolate. Add a layer of custard. Add a layer of bananas. Add a second layer of custard until it's level with the top of the crust. Garnish with shaved choclate. Fill a piping bag with the chantilly cream and pipe rosettes on top of the pie.

TO SERVE: Cut into wedges and place on individual plates.

WHITE CHOCOLATE CRÈME BRÛLÉE

7 oz white chocolate, chopped

2 cups whipping cream

½ cup milk

6 egg yolks

½ cup granulated or Demerara sugar

FOR ME, one of the most soothing, sexy and silky desserts is a well-made crème brûlée. Letting the mixture infuse overnight in the refrigerator results in a much creamier crème brûlée. Some people prefer a very thick sugar crust on top, but others prefer a thin one. Myself, I like a thin crust. *Serves 4 to 6*

Place chocolate in a bowl placed on top of a bowl of simmering water. Allow chocolate to melt and keep warm.

Place cream and milk in a saucepan on medium-high heat. Bring just to the boiling point, then remove from the stove. Whisk the cream mixture into the melted chocolate.

Fill a bowl with ice water and place another bowl on top of it. Place egg yolks in yet another bowl and temper (so that it doesn't curdle) and whisk while adding ¼ cup of the warm chocolate mixture. Slowly whisk in the remaining chocolate mixture. Pour into the bowl on top of the ice water and allow to cool. Cover and refrigerate overnight to allow the flavours to develop.

Preheat the oven to 250°F. Strain the chocolate mixture through a fine-mesh sieve and pour into four to six shallow ramekins or crème brûlée dishes, 6 inches in diameter.

Place the ramekins in a roasting pan, and add water to the pan until it reaches halfway up the sides of the ramekins. Bake in the oven for 45 minutes, or until your finger does not stick when you lightly press the centre of the crème brûlées. Remove from the oven and allow to cool. Refrigerate overnight to allow to set.

TO SERVE: Cover the top of each ramekin with sugar. Use a torch to caramelize the sugar, then allow the topping to cool before serving.

MOCHA ALMOND
FUDGE ICE CREAM

THIS IS probably one of the most popular flavours of ice cream that we've ever made. How can anyone resist mocha and almond *and* fudge? *Makes 1½ quarts*

CANDIED ALMONDS: Preheat the oven to 300°F. Line a baking sheet with parchment paper. Coarsely chop almonds and place in a bowl. Add simple syrup and toss well to coat evenly. Spread almonds over the baking sheet. Bake in the oven, stirring occasionally, for 15 to 20 minutes, or until sugar is dry.

FUDGE: Fill a bowl with ice water and place another bowl on top of it. Place sugar, cocoa, water and salt in a saucepan on high heat, whisking constantly while bringing the mixture to a boil. Remove from the stove. Strain the cocoa mixture through a fine-mesh sieve into the bowl on top of the ice water and allow to cool. Stir in vanilla.

ICE CREAM: Place chocolate in a bowl placed on top of a bowl of simmering water. Allow chocolate to melt and keep warm.

Place half of the sugar in the bottom of a saucepan, then add coffee, cream, milk and vanilla. Cook on medium heat until it just comes to a boil, then remove from the stove. Add melted chocolate and whisk until smooth.

Whisk together the remaining sugar and egg yolks in a bowl. Temper the egg mixture (so that it doesn't curdle) by whisking in ¼ cup of the warm chocolate mixture. Slowly whisk in the remaining warm chocolate mixture.

Transfer the mixture to a saucepan on medium heat and bring to 175°F (80 to 82°C) on a digital instant-read thermometer. Stir constantly and keep scraping the bottom of the pot with a spatula.

Fill a bowl with ice water and place another bowl on top of it. Pour the mixture into the bowl on top of the ice water and stir until completely cool. Cover and refrigerate overnight. Strain through a fine-mesh sieve. Place in an ice-cream maker and process according to the manufacturer's instructions.

When the ice cream is almost ready, stir in candied almonds. As you pack the ice cream into a storage container, layer it with swirls of fudge. Freeze until needed.

CANDIED ALMONDS

2 cups whole
blanched almonds

2 Tbsp simple syrup (page 137)

FUDGE

2 cups sugar

1½ cups cocoa powder

2 cups water

Pinch of salt

2 tsp vanilla extract

ICE CREAM

12 oz 33% milk chocolate,
chopped

¾ cup sugar

¼ cup crushed coffee beans

2½ cups whipping cream

3 cups milk

1 tsp vanilla extract

6 egg yolks

PEACHES
WITH BASIL

4 large freestone peaches,
peeled, pitted and sliced

4 Tbsp sugar

2 Tbsp white rum

1 Tbsp fresh lime juice

2 Tbsp thinly sliced
fresh basil leaves

6 sprigs fresh basil, for garnish

ONE OF MY favourite fruits in the summer has to be fresh ripe peaches. When I was a kid, my mom just peeled them, cut them up, placed them in a bowl and sprinkled them with sugar. I've made it a bit more grown up by adding rum, lime juice and basil. This the easiest of desserts to prepare and, in my opinion, one of the best. *Serves 4*

TO SERVE: Divide peach slices among four bowls. Sprinkle with sugar, rum, lime juice and basil leaves. Garnish each bowl with a sprig of basil.

STICKY TOFFEE PUDDING

WITH PEAR COMPOTE, CINNAMON MASCARPONE AND MAPLE SYRUP ICE CREAM

ICE CREAM

1½ cups whipping cream

½ cup maple syrup

1 tsp salt

¼ tsp vanilla extract

4 egg yolks

COMPOTE

2 Tbsp unsalted butter

6 Bosc or Anjou pears, peeled, cored and ¼-inch dice

⅓ cup granulated sugar

3 Tbsp brown sugar

1 vanilla bean, pulp only (page 10)

3 Tbsp brandy

1 lemon, juice only

MASCARPONE

½ cup whipping cream

1 Tbsp icing sugar

Pinch of ground cinnamon

½ vanilla bean, pulp only

1½ Tbsp honey

½ of a 250-g tub of mascarpone

DON'T LET the length of this recipe fool you; it's worth every minute. This classic dessert will thrill your guests. The combination of moist pudding, warm gooey toffee sauce, rich maple syrup ice cream and spicy cinnamon mascarpone puts this dish in a class by itself. *Serves 5 to 6*

ICE CREAM: Combine cream, maple syrup, salt and vanilla in a saucepan on medium-high heat. Cook for about 10 minutes, or until just simmering. Remove from the stove.

Whisk egg yolks until fluffy in a bowl. Temper the egg mixture (so that it doesn't curdle) by whisking in ¼ cup of the warm cream mixture. Slowly whisk in the remaining warm cream mixture.

Transfer to a saucepan on medium heat and bring to 175°F (80 to 82°C) on a digital instant-read thermometer. Stir constantly and keep scraping the bottom of the pot with a spatula.

Fill a bowl with ice water and place another bowl on top of it. Strain the mixture through a fine-mesh sieve into the bowl on top of the water and stir until cool. Cover and refrigerate overnight. Place in an ice-cream maker and process according to the manufacturer's instructions. Freeze until needed.

COMPOTE: Line a baking sheet with parchment paper. Melt butter in a large frying pan on medium-high heat. Add pears and sauté for 5 to 7 minutes, or until golden brown. Add granulated sugar, brown sugar and vanilla, then toss until diced pear is evenly coated. Cook for 5 to 7 minutes, or until dark golden brown. Add brandy and lemon juice, then cook for 1 minute.

Remove from the stove, then spread out diced pear on the prepared baking sheet and allow to cool. (Be sure to put parchment paper on the baking sheet or you can get off-flavours.) Transfer to an airtight container and refrigerate until needed.

MASCARPONE: Place a bowl in the freezer to chill. Add cream, icing sugar, cinnamon and vanilla to the chilled bowl. Whip until soft peaks form. Add honey and mix well. Slowly whisk in mascarpone a little at a time. Continue to whisk until stiff peaks form. Cover and refrigerate until needed.

TOFFEE SAUCE: Fill a bowl with ice water and place another bowl on top of it. Combine brown sugar, butter and cream in a saucepan on medium heat, stirring occasionally. When the sauce reaches a boil, remove from the stove. Pour the toffee into the bowl on top of the ice water and allow to cool.

PUDDING: Preheat the oven to 350°F. Butter 5 to 6 individual ramekins, 3 inches in diameter, and line the bottoms with parchment paper.

Place figs and boiling water in bowl, then allow to soak for 10 minutes. Take figs out of the water and save the soaking liquid. Chop figs into ¼-inch dice.

Sift together flour, baking powder and baking soda into a bowl.

Cream together butter, brown sugar and vanilla in a kitchen mixer with a paddle attachment. Add egg and mix well. Slowly add one third of the flour mixture and mix well. Add one third of the reserved soaking liquid and mix well. Alternate adding and mixing in the flour mixture and the soaking liquid until they're all used up. Add figs and mix until evenly distributed.

Spoon 2 Tbsp of the toffee sauce into the bottom of each ramekin. Add the fig mixture until the ramekins are three-quarters full. Place the ramekins on a baking sheet and bake in the oven for 30 to 40 minutes, or until puffed and dark golden brown. Remove from the oven and allow to cool. Refrigerate until needed.

TO SERVE: In a saucepan on low heat, reheat the remaining toffee sauce until runny.

Invert and unmould the individual toffee puddings onto a plate, then reheat in a microwave for 30 to 40 seconds on high. Spoon a generous amount of warmed toffee sauce over them.

Divide pear compote among plates, placing two dollops beside each pudding. Place 2 Tbsp of the cinnamon mascarpone on top of one dollop of pear compote and place 2 Tbsp of the maple syrup ice cream on top of the other.

TOFFEE SAUCE

1 cup brown sugar
½ cup unsalted butter
½ cup whipping cream

PUDDING

¾ cup dried figs
1¼ cups boiling water
1¾ cups all-purpose flour
1½ tsp baking powder
½ tsp baking soda
¼ cup unsalted butter, softened
½ cup brown sugar
1 vanilla bean, pulp only
1 egg

CRAB PANNA COTTA

THIS DESSERT was the unusual and delicious finale to our winning meal on the *Iron Chef America* show. The dish was created by Wayne Harris, the sous chef at Lumière restaurant. *Serves 6 to 8*

SORBET: Combine lemon juice and simple syrup in a bowl. Place cream in a saucepan on medium-high heat and bring to a simmer, then add to the lemon-sugar mixture and stir. Remove from the stove, allow to cool and refrigerate until chilled. Place in an ice-cream machine and process according to the manufacturer's instructions. Freeze until needed.

PANNA COTTA: Pick through the crabmeat to remove bits of shell and refrigerate until needed.

Place gelatin leaves in a bowl and cover with cold water. Let sit for about 5 minutes, or until softened. Take gelatin out of the water and squeeze out any excess liquid.

Place lemon juice and simple syrup in a saucepan on medium-high heat and heat until steaming. Add gelatin leaves and stir until dissolved. Strain through a fine-mesh sieve into the warmed whipping cream (must be warm so it won't curdle from the lemon juice).

Place 2 Tbsp of the crabmeat in the bottom of each of 6 to 8 ramekins, 3 inches in diameter. Pour cream mixture on top of crabmeat to fill the ramekins. Place in the refrigerator for about 1 hour, or until set.

TO SERVE: Unmould panna cottas one at a time by running hot water over the outside of the ramekin, then turning it upside down into your hand. Place a panna cotta in the centre of each chilled plate. Arrange diced pineapple beside the panna cotta. Place a scoop of lemon sorbet on top of the pineapple.

SORBET

1 cup fresh lemon juice

⅔ cup simple syrup (page 137)

1 cup whipping cream

PANNA COTTA

8 oz Dungeness crabmeat, shredded

2½ leaves gelatin

½ cup fresh lemon juice

¼ cup simple syrup

1⅓ cups whipping cream, warmed

½ fresh pineapple, peeled, cored and ¼-inch dice

FEENIE'S
CHOCOLATE TRIO

THIS DESSERT TRIO is a chocolate lover's dream: Milk Chocolate Panna Cotta with Chocolate Pecan Tuiles, Pecan Shortbread with Cocoa Cinnamon Sorbet, Caramel Chocolate Tart with Chocolate Topping. There are a lot of steps, but this dessert is not complicated and much of it can be made ahead. And it is really worth the effort!

A Silpat is a nonstick, washable, reusable liner for a baking sheet. Sometimes you can use parchment paper instead, but not in this case. *Serves 8*

MILK CHOCOLATE PANNA COTTA WITH
CHOCOLATE PECAN TUILES

PANNA COTTA: Place gelatin leaves in a bowl and cover with cold water. Let sit for about 3 to 5 minutes, until softened. Take gelatin out of the water and squeeze out any excess liquid.

Place milk, cream and sugar in a saucepan on high heat and bring just to a boil, then remove from the heat. Stir in gelatin.

Fill a bowl with ice water and place another bowl on top of it. Place chocolate in yet another bowl. Pour the warm milk mixture over chocolate and whisk in as chocolate melts. Strain chocolate mixture through a fine-mesh sieve into the bowl placed on top of the bowl of ice water. Allow to cool to room temperature. Whisk in vanilla, then pour into eight 2-oz stainless steel timbale moulds. Refrigerate for about 90 minutes, or until set. Will keep for 2 to 3 days in the refrigerator.

TUILES: Preheat the oven to 300°F. Spread out pecans on a baking sheet and toast in the oven for 20 minutes, or until brown but not burned. Allow to cool, then grind in a blender.

Combine ½ cup of the ground pecans (you will use the rest for the pecan shortbread), sugar, flour and cocoa in a bowl. In another bowl, mix together melted butter, lemon juice and brandy. Whisk the butter mixture into the pecan mixture. Cover and refrigerate the dough for at least 2 hours.

Preheat the oven to 350°F. Line a baking sheet with a Silpat. Make a triangle-shaped stencil for the tuiles by cutting out a triangle 1½ inches on each side, using the clean lid of a yogurt or sour cream container. Use a small metal spatula to spread the dough on the prepared baking sheet. Use the stencil to cut out tuiles, you should be able to make at least 8 to 10. Bake in the oven for 4 to 5 minutes, or until slightly brown around the edges. Remove from the oven and allow tuiles to cool completely before taking them off the Silpat.

PECAN SHORTBREAD
WITH COCOA CINNAMON SORBET

SHORTBREAD: Combine flour, ground pecans and salt in a bowl.

In a kitchen mixer with a paddle attachment, cream together butter, icing sugar and vanilla until light and fluffy. With the mixer on slow speed, add the flour mixture all at once and mix into a dough. Cover and refrigerate the dough for at least 3 hours.

Preheat the oven to 350°F. Line a baking sheet with parchment paper.

Roll out the dough between two sheets of parchment paper to a thickness of ⅛ to ¼ inch. Use a 2-inch diameter cookie cutter to cut out as many rounds as you can. Place the cookies on the prepared baking sheet, pierce them with a fork and sprinkle with sugar. Bake in the oven for about 7 minutes, or until light brown and crisp. Remove from the oven and allow to cool.

SORBET: Combine brown sugar, cocoa and water in a saucepan on high heat. Bring to a boil, then decrease the heat to low and simmer for 5 minutes. Remove from the stove, then whisk in chocolate, vanilla and cinnamon until smooth.

Fill a bowl with ice water and place another bowl on top of it. Strain the chocolate mixture through a fine-mesh sieve into the bowl on top of the ice water and allow to cool to room temperature. Cover and refrigerate overnight. Place in an ice-cream maker and process according to the manufacturer's instructions. Freeze until needed.

SHORTBREAD

1 cup all-purpose flour

½ cup toasted ground pecans

½ tsp salt

½ cup butter

⅓ cup icing sugar

1 tsp vanilla extract

2 Tbsp turbinado or coarse raw sugar

SORBET

1 cup packed brown sugar

⅔ cup cocoa powder

2½ cups water

1 oz 66% dark chocolate, chopped

1 tsp vanilla extract

2 tsp ground cinnamon

SHORTCRUST

½ cup butter

½ cup icing sugar

1 egg yolk

1 tsp orange zest

1 tsp ground cardamom

½ tsp vanilla extract

1¼ cups all-purpose flour

¼ cup cocoa powder

CARAMEL SAUCE

¼ cup water

1 cup sugar

1 tsp corn syrup

⅓ cup whipping cream

¼ cup butter

TOPPING

2½ cups 66% dark chocolate, chopped

2 cups whipping cream

2 Tbsp corn syrup

1 Tbsp brandy

Maldon salt or fleur de sel, for garnish

SHORTCRUST: Cream together butter and icing sugar in a kitchen mixer with a paddle attachment until light and fluffy. Mix in egg yolk, orange zest, cardamom and vanilla.

Sift together flour and cocoa into a bowl. With the mixer on slow speed, add all at once to the butter mixture, and mix into a dough. Cover and refrigerate the dough for at least 2 hours.

Butter 8 tart shells, 1 inch in diameter. Roll out the dough on a lightly floured surface to a thickness of ¼ inch. Use a 2-inch diameter cookie cutter to cut out 8 rounds. Press the dough into the prepared tart shells, then place them in the freezer for 10 minutes.

Preheat the oven to 350°F. Place the tart shells on a baking sheet and bake in the oven for 5 to 7 minutes, or until cooked through. Remove from the oven and allow to cool.

CARAMEL SAUCE: Place water, sugar and corn syrup in a saucepan on high heat and cook for about 10 minutes, or until amber in colour. Decrease the heat to low, then carefully whisk in cream. Whisk in butter, then increase the heat to high and bring back to a boil.

Fill a bowl with ice water and place a bowl on top of it. Strain the caramel sauce through a fine-mesh sieve into the bowl on top of the ice water and allow to cool to room temperature.

TOPPING: Place chocolate in a heatproof bowl. Place cream and corn syrup in a saucepan on high heat and bring to a boil, then pour over chocolate. As chocolate melts, whisk from the centre outward. Whisk in brandy. Place a sheet of plastic wrap directly on the surface of the mixture so that a skin does not form. Allow to cool but do not refrigerate.

TO ASSEMBLE: Spoon caramel sauce into the tart shells until half full. Refrigerate for about 30 minutes, or until set. Spoon chocolate topping into each tart shell until full. Refrigerate for about 30 minutes, or until set. The tarts will keep for 2 days, uncovered, in the refrigerator.

Refrigerate any extra chocolate topping to use as warm chocolate sauce. Will keep for 2 weeks.

TO SERVE: Unmould panna cottas one at a time by running hot water over the outside of the timbale mould, then turning it upside down into your hand. Place a panna cotta in the centre of each of eight chilled plates.

Place a shortbread and a tart (anchor the tart with a dab of warmed chocolate sauce) on each plate. Place a scoop of sorbet on top of each shortbread and insert a tuile in each panna cotta. Garnish each tart with a couple of grains of salt.

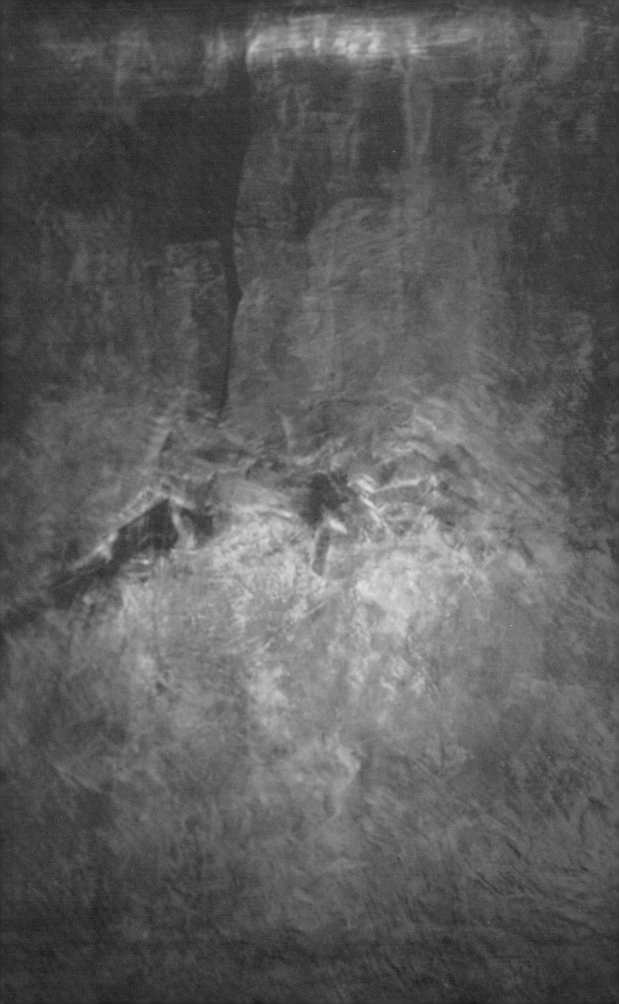

FEENIE'S THE BASICS

DARK CHICKEN OR DUCK STOCK

3 lbs fresh chicken (or duck) backs,
necks and a few wings

1 Tbsp vegetable oil

1 carrot, coarsely chopped

1 onion, coarsely chopped

2 cloves garlic, cut in half

1 stalk celery, coarsely chopped

3 sprigs fresh thyme

2 bay leaves

10 whole black peppercorns

Preheat the oven to 450°F. Rinse the backs, necks and wings thoroughly under cold running water for 5 to 10 minutes, or until water runs clear. Cut off and discard fatty skin.

Heat vegetable oil in a large roasting pan on high heat. Add chicken (or duck) pieces and roast in the oven for about 45 minutes, or until light brown. Make sure they do not burn, or the stock will taste bitter.

Add carrot, onion, garlic and celery. Return to the oven for another 30 minutes, or until chicken (or duck) turns dark brown and vegetables are caramelized. Pour off and discard fat.

Transfer roasted chicken (or duck) parts and vegetables to a stockpot on the stove-top on medium heat. Add a little cold water and stir to deglaze the bottom of the pan. Pour into the stockpot.

Add enough cold water to the stockpot to cover chicken (or duck) and vegetables. Add thyme, bay leaves and peppercorns. Increase the heat to high and bring to a boil. Decrease the heat to medium-low and gently simmer for 3 to 4 hours, or until rich golden brown.

Frequently skim off and discard fat and impurities that rise to the top.

Remove from the stove and strain through a fine-mesh sieve into a clean container and allow to cool. Stock can be used as is, but for more intense flavour, reduce to half on low heat.

Can be used right away. Will keep in the refrigerator for up to 1 week or in the freezer for up to 2 months. *Makes about 8 cups, or 4 cups reduced*

WHITE CHICKEN STOCK

5 lbs fresh chicken bones, backs and necks

1 large carrot, coarsely chopped

1 leek, white part only, finely chopped

1 onion, coarsely chopped

2 stalks celery, coarsely chopped

5 cloves garlic

2 sprigs fresh thyme

2 bay leaves

Rinse chicken bones, backs and necks thoroughly under cold running water for 5 to 10 minutes, or until water runs clear. Cut off and discard fatty skin. Place chicken in a large stockpot and cover with cold water. On medium heat, bring to a boil. Decrease the heat to low and simmer, uncovered, for 20 minutes, frequently skimming off and discarding the fat and impurities that rise to the surface.

Add all the remaining ingredients and simmer, uncovered, on low heat, for 2 hours. To ensure a clear stock, do not allow to boil. Frequently skim off and discard fat and impurities that rise to the top.

Remove from the stove and strain through a fine-mesh sieve into a clean container. Allow to cool. Cover and refrigerate. Once the stock has been refrigerated for a few hours, the fat rises to the top and hardens, making it easy to remove and discard.

Can be used right away. Will keep in the refrigerator for up to 4 days or in the freezer for up to 3 months.

Makes about 16 cups

SHELLFISH STOCK

6 lobster (or crab) shells

3 Tbsp butter

2 carrots, diced

2 stalks celery, diced

1 onion, diced

2 sprigs fresh thyme

4 bay leaves

1 head garlic, cut in half sideways

8 black peppercorns

2 Tbsp tomato paste

3 quarts water

Preheat the oven to 400°F. Place lobster (or crab) shells in a roasting pan and cook in the oven for 20 to 25 minutes, or until browned and dry but not burned.

Melt butter in stockpot on medium to medium-high heat. Add carrots, celery and onion, then sauté for about 5 minutes, until onions are translucent. Add thyme, bay leaves, garlic, peppercorns and tomato paste. Add the roasted lobster (or crab) shells. Add water and bring to a simmer. Decrease the heat to medium and simmer, uncovered for

45 minutes. Frequently skim off and discard impurities that rise to the top.

Strain stock into a clean saucepan on high heat, then cook until reduced to 1 quart. Season with salt and freshly ground pepper. Allow to cool and refrigerate or freeze until needed. Will keep in the refrigerator for 1 week or in the freezer for 1 month.

Makes 1 quart

BEEF STOCK

2 lbs beef bones

3 carrots, cut in chunks

2 onions, cut in chunks

4 stalks celery, cut in chunks

1 head garlic, cut in half

5 sprigs fresh thyme

1 bay leaf

10 black peppercorns

Preheat the oven to 450°F. Lightly grease two roasting pans with a bit of vegetable oil. Arrange bones in a single layer in one pan and roast in the oven, turning occasionally, for 1 to 1½ hours, or until dark brown. At the same time, place carrots, onions, celery and garlic in the other pan and roast in the oven for 45 to 60 minutes, or until caramelized. Remove bones and vegetables from the oven when done.

Pour off and discard fat from the pan of bones. Place both pans on the stove-top on medium heat. Add a little water to both pans and stir to deglaze the bottoms.

Transfer the contents of both pans to a stockpot. Add thyme, bay leaf and peppercorns. Add enough cold water to cover ingredients. On medium heat, simmer, uncovered, for 3 to 4 hours. Frequently skim off and discard impurities that rise to the surface. Keep the stock ingredients at least three-quarters covered with water, adding more cold water as needed. Remove from the stove and allow to cool slightly.

Strain through a fine-mesh sieve into a clean container. For more intense flavour, cook over low heat until stock is reduced to half. Cool to room temperature and refrigerate. Remove and discard the cap of fat on the stock.

Can be used right away. Will keep in the refrigerator for up to 1 week or in the freezer for up to 3 months.

Makes 8 to 10 cups, or 4 to 5 cups reduced

VEAL STOCK

1 lb milk-fed veal bones (shank if possible)

⅓ cup honey

⅓ cup unsalted butter

1 carrot, coarsely chopped

1 leek, white part only, coarsely chopped

½ onion, peeled and chopped

1 stalk celery, coarsely chopped

5 cloves garlic, peeled and minced

1 Tbsp tomato paste

1 tomato, peeled, deseeded and chopped

2 sprigs fresh thyme

1 bay leaf

Preheat the oven to 450°F. Place bones in a large roasting pan and roast in the oven for 30 to 35 minutes, or until lightly browned. Pour off and discard excess fat from the pan, then roast bones for another 10 minutes.

Melt honey and butter in a saucepan on medium heat. Pour honey mixture over bones and roast for another 5 minutes. Transfer bones to a large stockpot and set aside. Leave the oven on.

Place carrot, leek, onion, celery and garlic in the same roasting pan in which you roasted the bones. Roast vegetables in the oven or cook on medium-high heat on the stove-top for about 10 minutes, or until golden brown. Add 2 cups cold water and bring to a boil, stirring to deglaze the bottom of the pan. Cook until reduced to half. Add to bones in the stockpot. Add tomato paste, tomato, thyme and bay leaf.

Add enough cold water to cover bones. On low heat, simmer for 6 to 8 hours (do not allow to boil). Frequently skim off and discard fat and impurities that rise to the top. Keep the stock ingredients at least three-quarters covered with water, adding more cold water as needed.

Remove from the stove and allow to cool slightly. Strain through a fine-mesh sieve into a clean container.

Can be used right away. Will keep in the refrigerator for up to 1 week or in the freezer for up to 3 months.

Makes about 5 cups

VEGETABLE STOCK

1 bulb fennel, thinly sliced

1 onion, peeled and thinly sliced

2 stalks celery, thinly sliced

1 carrot, thinly sliced

1 leek, thinly sliced

1 tomato, roughly chopped

4 cloves garlic, peeled

1 tsp whole white peppercorns

3 sprigs fresh thyme

1-inch piece fresh ginger, sliced

5 cups water

Combine all the ingredients in a stock-pot on medium heat and bring to a boil. Decrease the heat to low and sim-mer for 30 to 45 minutes. Frequently skim off and discard impurities that rise to the top.

Remove from the stove and strain through a fine-mesh sieve, lightly press-ing solids to extract as much liquid as possible.

Can be used right away. Will keep in the refrigerator for up to 1 week or in the freezer for up to 2 months.

Makes about 4 cups

RENDERED DUCK FAT

4 lbs duck fat, in 1-inch pieces

1 cup water

Never throw away duck or goose used in cooking, for it can be reused. Melt the fat, then strain through a fine-mesh sieve and pour into airtight containers.

Place fat and water in a saucepan and cook on low heat for about 45 min-utes, or until fat melts and the water has evaporated. Remove from the stove and allow to cool for 10 minutes. Strain through a fine-mesh sieve into airtight containers. Will keep in the refrigerator for up to 3 weeks or in the freezer for up to 1 year.

Makes about 4 cups

PEKING DUCK BROTH

If you make the Peking Duck Terrine with Mandarin Pancake (page 74), you will end up with 2 Peking duck carcasses, exactly what you need to make this broth. This broth also serves as a great sauce for Corn, Caramelized Onion and Chanterelle Ravioli (page 38).

NUOC CHAM DRESSING

4 Tbsp + 2 tsp nuoc cham

(Vietnamese fish sauce)

5 Tbsp water

2 pieces lemon grass, each 1-inch long

1 small clove garlic, roughly chopped

1 Thai chili (page 24), deseeded and chopped

4 Tbsp palm sugar (Asian food stores)

PEKING DUCK BROTH

4 Tbsp canola oil

1 onion, ½-inch dice

½ carrot, ½-inch dice

2 ribs celery, ½-inch dice

2 carcasses of Chinese barbecued ducks

2 Tbsp dark soy sauce

2 Tbsp nuoc cham dressing

2 Tbsp oyster sauce

1 Tbsp ginger, roughly chopped

½ stalk lemon grass, crushed, 1-inch lengths

1 Tbsp coriander seeds

1 Tbsp black peppercorns

½ orange, zest only

5 quarts water

NUOC CHAM DRESSING: Combine all the ingredients in a saucepan on medium-high heat and bring to a boil. Cook until reduced by half (be sure to keep an eye on it as this is a very small amount and will reduce quickly). Remove from the stove and allow to cool. Strain through a fine-mesh sieve and discard the solids.

PEKING DUCK BROTH: Heat oil in a stockpot on medium heat and sauté for about 15 minutes, or until well caramelized. Add the remaining ingredients, increase the heat to high, and bring to a boil. Decrease the heat to low and simmer for at least 2 hours. Remove from the heat. Strain through a fine-mesh sieve and discard the solids. Will keep in the freezer for 4 months.

Makes about 3 quarts

CLARIFIED BUTTER

2 cups unsalted butter

Place butter in the top of a double boiler over boiling water on medium-high heat. Cook for about 10 minutes, until butter separates and milk solids appear. Skim off and discard any white foam that forms on the surface. Remove from the stove and allow to cool for 10 minutes. Place in the refrigerator until butter hardens.

Use the handle of a serving spoon to make a small hole in the top of the hardened butter. Carefully pour away and discard water and milk solids.

Place clarified butter in an airtight container. Will keep in the refrigerator for up to 1 week. To use, melt clarified butter as needed.

Makes about 1½ cups

MAYONNAISE

1 egg yolk
1 Tbsp rice vinegar
½ tsp fresh lemon juice
1 tsp Dijon mustard
1 cup grapeseed oil

Combine egg yolk, vinegar, lemon juice and mustard in a food processor or blender on medium speed. With the motor running, slowly drizzle in grapeseed oil in a steady stream. Transfer to an airtight container. Will keep in the refrigerator for up to 1 week.

Makes about 1 cup

CRÈME FRAÎCHE

Many specialty food stores do sell crème fraîche, but you can make a good substitute at home. Crème fraîche is a great addition to sauces or soups, but it must be put in at the last minute and should not be boiled. It's also a delicious accompaniment to fresh fruit and desserts in place of whipped cream.

1 cup whipping cream
⅓ cup buttermilk
1 tsp fresh lemon juice

Combine all the ingredients in a glass jar. Cover and let stand at room temperature in a warm (not hot) place for 8 to 24 hours, or until very thick. Give it a shake every hour or so to keep it from breaking up. When it looks ready, give it a good stir, cover and refrigerate. Will keep in the refrigerator for up to 1 week.

Makes about 1⅓ cups

TOMATO CONCASSÉ

Fill a bowl with ice water. Bring a pot of water to a boil on high heat. Add whole tomatoes and blanch them for about 10 to 20 seconds (the riper the tomatoes, the less blanching time needed). Use a slotted spoon to remove tomatoes from the boiling water and immediately plunge them into the ice water to stop the cooking. Allow tomatoes to cool for about 1 minute.

Remove tomatoes from the ice water. Use a small paring knife to remove the tomato cores. Peel tomatoes and cut in half. Use a small spoon to gently scoop out the centre flesh or gently squeeze out seeds (keep the centre flesh to make tomato sauce or to add to stocks or soups). Cut tomatoes into ¼-inch dice. Will keep in an airtight container in the refrigerator for no longer than 1 day.

CILANTRO OR BASIL OIL

CILANTRO OIL
1 cup fresh cilantro
½ cup fresh Italian (flat-leaf) parsley
1 cup grapeseed oil

BASIL OIL
3 cups fresh basil leaves
1 cup grapeseed oil

Fill a bowl with ice water. Bring a pot of water to a boil. Blanch herbs by placing them in the boiling water for about 10 seconds, just till they wilt. Take out herbs and immediately plunge them into the ice water. Drain herbs, then thoroughly dry them between two towels.

Purée herbs in a blender, then slowly add grapeseed oil and incorporate.

Transfer to an airtight container and refrigerate overnight to infuse. Strain through a cheesecloth-lined sieve and discard herbs. Will keep in the refrigerator for up to 2 months in an airtight container.

Makes about 1 cup

SIMPLE SYRUP

2 cups granulated sugar
1½ cups water

Combine sugar and water in a saucepan on medium-high heat and bring to a boil. Continue to boil for 2 minutes. Remove from the stove and strain through a fine-mesh sieve. Allow to cool. Store at room temperature in an airtight container. Will keep for up to 10 days.

Makes about 2 cups

PASTA DOUGH WITH SEMOLINA

14 oz all-purpose flour

14 oz semolina

Pinch of salt

16 large egg yolks

1 to 4 whole eggs

1½ tsp olive oil

1 whole egg, beaten

½ tsp water

2 eggs, beaten, for egg wash

Place flour, semolina and salt in the bowl of a heavy-duty kitchen mixer with a dough hook. On a slow speed, incorporate egg yolks one at a time, followed by 1 whole egg. Test the dough by squeezing some of the mixture in your hand. If it stays together, do not add more whole eggs. If it does not stay together, incorporate 1 more whole egg and test. Keep adding and testing 1 whole egg at a time as needed until the dough is ready.

When the dough is ready, add oil and knead. It should form a dough that is not too wet or too sticky. If the mixture is too liquid, add more flour.

Gently knead dough on a lightly floured surface and form into two cylinders that are 3 inches thick. Cut each cylinder into four equal portions, wrap each portion in plastic wrap and refrigerate for 1 hour before using.

TO ASSEMBLE RAVIOLI: Roll out each portion of pasta dough in a pasta machine, according to the manufacturer's instructions. Each sheet should be about ¹⁄₁₆ inch thick and large enough to cover a ravioli mould. As the sheets of dough are rolled out, cover them with a clean tea towel so they won't dry out. Make 8 to 10 sheets of pasta.

Sprinkle the inside of the ravioli mould with a little flour to prevent sticking. Line the mould with 1 sheet of pasta, pressing gently into the spaces. Place the filling in a pastry bag with a round flat tip and pipe about 1 Tbsp (or a bit less, you have to be careful that the dough does not tear) into each square in the ravioli mould.

Place another sheet of pasta on a clean surface, then brush one side of it with beaten egg. Carefully place the pastry sheet, egg wash side down, over the filled ravioli. Gently press along the seams to ensure the egg wash seals the pasta sheets together and also to get rid of any air bubbles. Use a floured rolling pin to gently roll over the top sheet. This will help to mould and separate the individual ravioli.

Trim off the outside edges and discard any trimmings. Allow to rest for 20 minutes. Each mould makes 10 ravioli for a total of 40 to 50 pieces of ravioli.

The ravioli can be made ahead up to this point. If you are making them ahead, turn over the mould onto a parchment-lined baking sheet and remove all the ravioli in one piece from the mould. Place the entire sheet of ravioli in the freezer. Repeat until all the pasta dough is used up. After being frozen, the ravioli in each sheet will break apart easily. No cutting is necessary if done properly. Place ravioli pieces in an airtight container; will keep in the freezer for up to 2½ weeks. Do not thaw before cooking.

METRIC CONVERSIONS

(rounded off to the nearest even whole number)

WEIGHT			VOLUME	
IMPERIAL OR U.S.	METRIC		IMPERIAL OR U.S.	METRIC
1 oz	30 g		⅛ tsp	0.5 mL
2 oz	60 g		¼ tsp	1 mL
3 oz	85 g		½ tsp	2.5 mL
4 oz	115 g		¾ tsp	4 mL
5 oz	140 g		1 tsp	5 mL
6 oz	170 g		1 Tbsp	15 mL
7 oz	200 g		1½ Tbsp	23 mL
8 oz (½ lb)	225 g		⅛ cup	30 mL
9 oz	255 g		¼ cup	60 mL
10 oz	285 g		⅓ cup	80 mL
11 oz	310 g		½ cup	120 mL
12 oz	340 g		⅔ cup	160 mL
13 oz	370 g		¾ cup	180 mL
14 oz	400 g		1 cup	240 mL
15 oz	425 g			
16 oz (1 lb)	455 g			
2 lbs	910 g			

IMPERIAL OR U.S.	METRIC
⅛ inch	3 mm
¼ inch	6 mm
½ inch	12 mm
¾ inch	2 cm
1 inch	2.5 cm
1¼ inches	3 cm
1½ inches	3.5 cm
1¾ inches	4.5 cm
2 inches	5 cm
3 inches	7.5 cm
4 inches	10 cm
5 inches	12.5 cm
6 inches	15 cm
7 inches	18 cm
12 inches	30 cm
24 inches	60 cm

BAKING UTENSILS

IMPERIAL OR U.S.	METRIC
5 × 9-inch loaf pan	2 L loaf pan
9 × 13-inch cake pan	4 L cake pan
11 × 17-inch baking sheet	30 × 45-cm baking sheet

OVEN TEMPERATURE

IMPERIAL OR U.S.	METRIC
150°F	65°C
250°F	120°C
275°F	135°C
300°F	150°C
325°F	160°C
350°F	180°C
375°F	190°C
400°F	200°C
425°F	220°C
450°F	230°C

LIQUID MEASURES (FOR ALCOHOL)

IMPERIAL OR U.S.	METRIC
1 oz	30 mL
1½ oz	45 mL
2 oz	60 mL
3 oz	90 mL
4 oz	120 mL

ACKNOWLEDGEMENTS

THIS BOOK was a joy to put together, and I have a lot of people to thank for making it possible.

Nicole Arnett, my assistant and marketing director. She is a gifted young lady and always a joy to work with—even when we are on a deadline. I would like to thank her for staying two steps ahead of me at all times.

Marc-Andre Choquette, my chef de cuisine of both Lumière and Feenie's and a man of unshakable concentration. He runs a tight ship in our kitchens, and I always know that the restaurants are in great hands when he is around. I am very fortunate to have such a talented individual as my right-hand man.

Wayne Harris, my sous chef at Lumière. This man has nerves of steel; if you saw him in action on *Iron Chef America,* you know what I mean. He is quite simply a great guy to know and to work with every day.

Colleen McClean, my head chef at Feenie's. She has been tireless in her efforts to keep the menus at Feenie's fresh and exciting. It is great to have her back here with us. My thanks to her for her patience with me and this project.

My mentors, Michel Jacob, Daniel Boulud, Emile Jung, and Johnny Letzer. Each of these talented men has been an inspiration to me throughout my career. I would like to thank them for their generosity in welcoming me into their kitchens time and again and for showing me the wide world of truly fabulous European cuisine. Thank you, dear friends!

My entire team front and back who, night after night, turn these recipes into reality and make Feenie's such an extraordinary place.

INDEX